ESTES PARK

A Quick History

by Kenneth Jessen

J. V. Publications
2212 Flora Ct.
Loveland, Colorado 80537

© Copyright 1996 by Kenneth Jessen

All rights reserved, including those to reproduce this booklet, or parts thereof, in any form, without permission in writing from the publisher.

Second Edition
2 3 4 5 6 7 8 9

Printed in the United States of America

Cataloging:

    Jessen, Kenneth Christian
    Estes Park - A Quick History

    Bibliography
    Includes Index
1. Colorado - History - Estes Park. I. Title

Library of Congress Catalog Card Number

ISBN: 1-928656-00-5

Book design: Kenneth Jessen

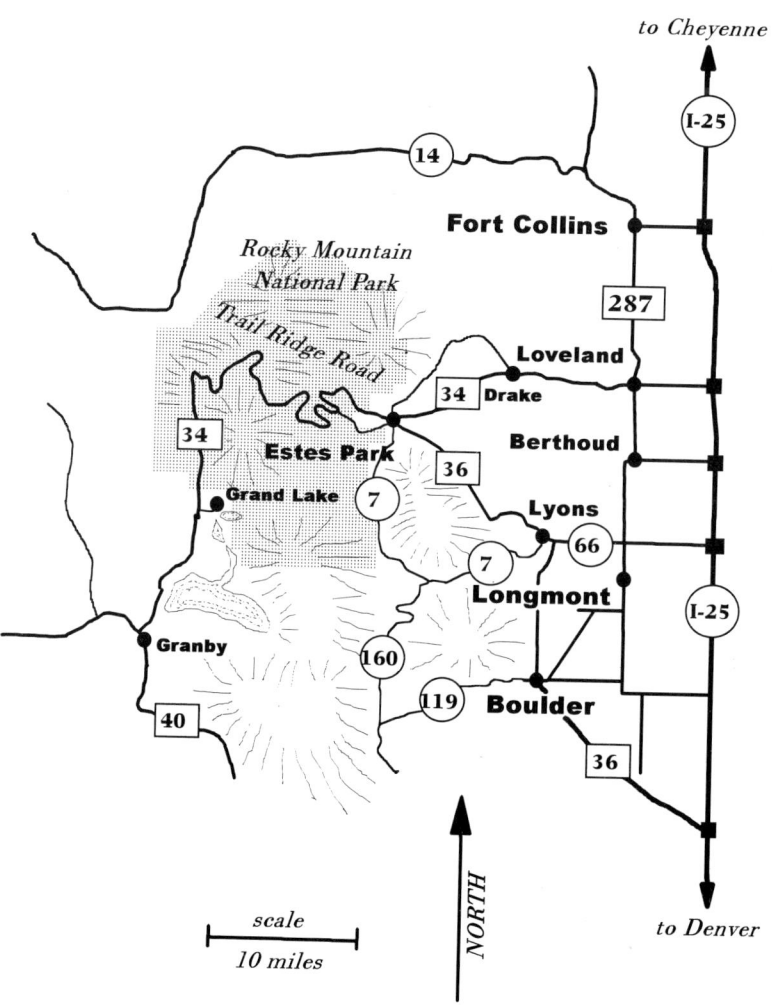

ACKNOWLEDGMENTS

Leland Feitz began this series of quick histories using his extensive knowledge of the Cripple Creek area ending with his latest booklet, *Conejos Country*. John Carr of the Estes Park Area Historical Museum contributed a great deal to this work by proof-reading the entire manuscript and providing the story on Hidden Valley. He was also helpful in locating photographs from the museum's collection. Enda Mills Kiley, daughter of Enos Mills, and Elizabeth M. Mills, granddaughter of Enos Mills, provided their inputs to the chapter on Enos Mills and also opened up the extensive Mills Cabin collection of photographs for use in this booklet. Joan Childers, Rocky Mountain National Park, helped clarify historical facts, read three of the historical sketches and assisted in gathering photographs of early lodges within the Park. Cathy Swan, Denver Public Library, helped gather photographs from the extensive collection within the Western History Department. This is an easy to read booklet. A great deal of the credit goes to professional writer Ron Williams. Susan Hoskinson performed the final proofreading in the book's typeset form.

Kenneth Jessen
Loveland, Colorado, 1996

TABLE OF CONTENTS

INTRODUCTION..vi
THE PARK'S FIRST SETTLER..1
THE FIRST ASCENTS OF LONGS PEAK.......................................5
LORD DUNRAVEN CONTROLS ESTES PARK...........................13
THE MURDER OF ROCKY MOUNTAIN JIM...............................17
THE FATHER OF ROCKY MOUNTAIN NATIONAL PARK........23
THE RILEY ROAD..31
STANLEY: HIS STEAMER AND HOTEL.....................................37
THE HIGHEST ROAD IN THE U.S...43
LODGES WITHIN ROCKY MOUNTAIN NATIONAL PARK........49
ESTES PARK VILLAGE..57
COLORADO'S WORST NATURAL DISASTER...........................61
THE LAWN LAKE TIME BOMB..69
HIDDEN VALLEY (by John Carr)...73
BIBLIOGRAPHY...77
INDEX...80
ABOUT THE AUTHOR..82

INTRODUCTION

The history of Estes Park is intertwined with the history of Rocky Mountain National Park; therefore, this booklet contains historical sketches of both areas.

The Estes Park valley was discovered by Native Americans probably thousands of years ago. They used Trail Ridge as a means of getting across the Continental Divide and left behind ample evidence of their passage. Encroachment by Europeans came during the 1800s, and by 1860, there was a permanent settler within Estes Park, namely Joel Estes and his family. At first, other settlers came to ranch and make a living off the land. The natural beauty and spectacular, rugged mountains soon attracted tourists. Some of them were drawn to climb the mountains, especially Longs Peak, while others simply came to enjoy the serene surroundings. Many settlers quickly discovered the lucrative recreational business and began constructing cottages and lodges. As better roads were built from towns along the base of the Front Range, the park experienced a steady growth.

The greatest milestone in the history of Estes Park area was the formation of Rocky Mountain National Park in 1915, an effort driven by naturalist Enos Mills. The village of Estes Park was an outgrowth of the popularity of Rocky Mountain National Park, and its economy evolved to service the many visitors.

While mankind today has continued to populate and develop Estes Park, the National Park Service has exercised a policy to depopulate Rocky Mountain National Park through the methodical removal of all lodges, cottages, service stations, stores, homesteads and other structures. So thorough has been their efforts that visitors today can hardly find a trace of some of the great commercial properties once located at Moraine Park, Horseshoe Park, Bear Lake and other locations.

The Estes Park area continues to make history. In 1976, Colorado's greatest natural disaster occurred just east of its city limits during the Big Thompson flood. Just six years later, Estes Park itself was hit by a flood caused by the failure of a dam located in a high remote valley within Rocky Mountain National Park. This began an era of dam removal from Rocky Mountain National Park to further restore it to its original, natural state.

This booklet concludes with an article written by John Carr on the economic failure and subsequent removal of the last major commercial enterprise within the park, the Hidden Valley Ski Area.

I sincerely hope you enjoy reading this booklet.

Kenneth Jessen, 1996

THE PARK'S FIRST SETTLER

There isn't any record of who the first white man was to set foot in Estes Park. It could have been a professional trapper sent by the Hudson Bay Company or the American Fur Company during the early 1800s. Virtually all streams flowing out of the eastern base of the Rocky Mountains had been explored by this time. Kit Carson may have entered Estes Park with a group of trappers and spent the winter of 1840-1841 trapping beaver. C.W. Buchholtz in his book, *Rocky Mountain National Park*, tempered this by saying, "It is possible Kit Carson and his sidekicks did explore all of the hidden valleys of Rocky Mountain National Park, but those claims might also be wishful thinking..."

One person who struggled with gold fever was Joel Estes. He was born in Kentucky and became a Missouri farmer. He and his wife Patsy raised no less than thirteen children. In 1849, Joel and his oldest son, Hardin, set out for California, with thousands of others in search of gold. Unlike the majority of prospectors, they staked out a profitable claim which they were able to sell for $30,000 during a time when men worked for $1.50 a day. This made the Estes family relatively rich. As the years passed, Joel could not control his wanderlust and returned to California and even ventured to Oregon. In 1859, news of the gold strike in the Pikes Peak region sent Joel, his wife, and his six children, still living at home, to Colorado.

The Estes family arrived in Denver on June 15, 1859, and scouted the area. Joel apparently was not impressed with the gold deposits found in the area streams after camping in Golden. He decided to take up ranching and settled near Fort Lupton where the family constructed some cabins. They mowed the native grass and put it up for the winter to feed their small herd.

Joel and his twelve-year-old son, Milton, went on a hunting trip that October in the mountains west of Fort Lupton. They traveled up a route that may have taken them along the St. Vrain or the Little Thompson rivers. Eventually, they climbed over a gentle rise and looked down into a valley or park which was totally unoccupied. They thought at first that this was North Park, but after a few days of exploration, realized it was some place new and unexplored. They found the remains of lodge poles left by Native Americans, but no signs of white man's presence. The place was a delight to behold with its lush meadows and majestic peaks.

Joel determined that this remote, high valley was going to be his home. In 1860, he moved his family to the park where he and his sons constructed two log cabins. They took possession of the land by "squatting" on it and were monarchs of all they could see. There weren't any laws to prohibit them nor any taxes to pay. Joel introduced a herd of around sixty cattle brought up from their Fort Lupton ranch. Joel hired several men to guard the cattle during the winter.

Joel was a very resourceful pioneer. He realized that raising cattle would be difficult at such a high altitude and began to harvest the abundant elk and deer. The demand for meat in Denver was quite high. Most of Denver's residents were miners preoccupied with the search for gold or silver and getting food was far from their minds. This allowed Joel to sell as much wild game and hides as he could kill and haul to Denver. Later, Milton Estes wrote that during one fall and winter, he personally killed one hundred elk, as well as other game animals, for his father. By 1863, Joel completed a primitive trail down from the park to allow him better access to Denver, a trip which they made every other month.

Life was harsh, especially during the winter. Hay had to be cut and put up during the short summer months. If the hay ran out, the cattle had to be moved to lower pastures. The periodic trips to Denver were not easy with the round trip requiring four days.

In August, 1864, William N. Byers, along with three companions, used the primitive trail to reach the park. Byers was the editor and founder of the *Rocky Mountain News* and had an adventurous spirit. During this trip, Byers met Joel Estes and one of his sons along the trail. Byers continued on to the cabins where he met Patsy and some of the other children. The family had not seen any other humans that year and welcomed the Byers party. The newspaper editor, no doubt, provided the Estes family with the latest news from the outside world. During the course of his exploration of the park, William Byers made an unsuccessful attempt to climb Longs Peak. When he returned to his office in Denver, he said this of the place, "Eventually, this park will become a favorite pleasure resort." In the process, he named it Estes Park after the hospitable family he had met.

It is one thing to be a summer tourist in Estes Park and enjoy the mountains, stay in a nice lodge, and eat in a comfortable restaurant, but quite another to be at the mercy of the elements. For the Estes family, however, the park was a constant struggle for survival. The winter of 1864-1865 was quite severe, and the family decided to move back down to the plains. Supposedly, Joel Estes sold his claim for a yoke of oxen. Joel may not have had any legal title to the land since he was a squatter. It was a spring day in April, 1866, when the Estes family made their way up Muggins Gulch and out of the park using the trail they had created. They never returned and went on to live out their lives ranching in mild southern Colorado.

Joel Estes moved his family to the Park in 1860 to become the first permanent settler. The Park was named for Joel by William Newton Byers, editor of the Rocky Mountain News. *(Estes Park Area Historical Museum)*

This photograph of lodgepoles in Estes Park was taken on Riverside Drive in 1905 and are firm evidence of the seasonal occupation by Native Americans. (Estes Park Area Historical Museum, E627)

THE FIRST ASCENTS OF LONGS PEAK

At 14,255 feet above sea level, Longs Peak and its sister, Mount Meeker, dominate the Estes Park skyline. Longs Peak has been the focus of attention ever since it was first spotted, and there has always been the question of who climbed the great mountain first? In 1914, the Colorado Mountain Club arranged to have two elders of the Arapahoe tribe return to Estes Park. There they were asked to recount living and hunting on the land which had been taken from them by white men. The elders, Sherman Sage and Gun Griswold, took a two-week pack trip around the park with an interpreter and two white companions.

The two Arapahoe men revealed the names of many of the features in the park and added a number of stories. Gun Griswold told of how his father, Old Man Gun, trapped eagles on the summit of Longs Peak. Gun was a medicine man of note as well as a warrior. To make a traditional headdress, he needed the revered eagle feathers. He climbed the mountain and dug a vertical pit where he could hide. Gun would climb the peak at night so that the eagles could not see him, and once in the hole, he would pull the pelt of a coyote over him. Tallow was used to give the pelt just the right smell. When a sharp-eyed, high flying eagle spotted what appeared to be a coyote, the bird would swoop down and dig its talons into the pelt. Old Man Gun would quickly grab the eagle with his herb-covered hand. The herbs rendered the eagle helpless allowing Gun to tie the birds feet and extract its feathers.

Gun Griswold continued his story and told his white companions that he and five other Arapahoe men climbed Longs Peak to check out the story. The climb was made in 1859 and sure enough, they found Old Man Gun's eagle trap. The hole had dirt scattered about. When the Powell party climbed the peak a decade later, no such hole was reported. However, frost heaving could have closed it. Also, the summit of Longs Peak is as big as a football field and such a feature could easily have been overlooked.

French trappers traveling through the area saw the twin peaks of Longs and Meeker, which at a distance, look the same height. They named the peaks Two Ears. Major Stephen Long is said to be the first to spot the great mountain on behalf of the U.S. Government on June 30, 1820. In reality, the entire expedition probably saw the mountain at the same time once they realized that what they believed to be distant clouds were really snow-capped peaks.

Joel Estes entered the park in 1859 and Alonzo Allen prospected for gold in a meadow southeast of Longs Peak in 1864. These settlers were aware of this great mountain, but no recorded climb was made for several years.

William Newton Byers was the founder and editor of the Rocky Mountain News. *He first saw Estes Park in 1864 on an unsuccessful attempt to climb Longs Peak. He visited the Estes family, the only settlers in the area, and named the park for them. (Colorado Historical Society F7362)*

William N. Byers, founder and editor the *Rocky Mountain News*, named Estes Park after its first permanent resident. Byers had his own ambitions to make the first ascent of Longs Peak. From the Boulder Field, Byers and a companion reached the top of the then unnamed Mount Meeker. They looked at the nasty ridge which connects Meeker and Longs and elected to retreat. As a side note, Byers recorded that they found a register on Mount Meeker containing five names, but failed to publish the names. Byers foolishly predicted that no man would ever reach the summit of Longs Peak.

One of the greatest American explorers was John Wesley Powell. He lost an arm fighting in the Civil War, but this didn't stop him from going west in 1867 on an expedition. He climbed Pikes Peak and returned the following year with a so-called scientific expedition. The expedition consisted of Powell's family and some volunteer college students. Powell hired a respected mountain man, Jack Sumner, to guide him to Longs Peak. This happened to be William Byer's brother-in-law, and when Byers got wind of the expedition, he joined Powell. At the time, Byers may have wanted to redeem himself after his previous defeat.

In August, a base camp was set up at Grand Lake. After two days of riding east through untouched, untamed territory, the party reached the foot of McHenry's Peak. They climbed the ridge which connects McHenry's with Chiefs Head. Next, they walked over the top of Chiefs Head and encountered the knife-edge ridge leading over Pagoda to Longs Peak. This forced them to retreat. Maybe Byers was correct and the peak could not be climbed.

This time the party went over the Continental Divide to Wild Basin and camped above Sandbeach Lake. They arrived late in the afternoon, and one of the students, L.W. Keplinger, volunteered to reconnoiter the route above the camp. He managed to get around a couple of tight places and arrived above the East Face just 200 feet from the summit. Alone, on a very exposed place with nothing but a thousand feet of air below, with night approaching, Keplinger lost his nerve and returned to camp. He could have been credited with the first recorded ascent of Longs Peak.

The next morning, the men climbed the peak and arrived on the summit at 10 a.m., August 23, 1868. After building a rock monument and christening it, the Powell party spent three hours gathering specimens, to lend validity to the fact that this was a scientific expedition. After his successful first recorded ascent of Long Peak, Powell went on to explore the Colorado River and run the numerous rapids in Grand Canyon

In 1871, using rather poor judgment, Rev. Elkanah Lamb first made a solo climb of Longs Peak followed by the first descent of the East Face via the Notch Couloir, the Broadway Ledge, and finally down the steep ice of the upper portion of the Mills Glacier. Lamb lost his footing and nearly slid to his death which later prompted naming this feature The Lambs Slide. (Estes Park Area Historical Museum EP911)

Once Longs Peak had been climbed, others also wanted to follow, and the peak became a focal point for many climbing attempts. Donald Brown made the first ascent via the Keyhole route, the most popular route on the mountain today. World famous geologist Clarence King joined Henry Adams to make a successful ascent in 1871. A preacher named Elkanah Lamb put together a small party that same year to climb Longs Peak. They selected the Keyhole route, but Lamb's climbing partners gave up before reaching the Keyhole itself. Lamb trudged on alone along the traverse and up the Trough to the summit. Once on top, Lamb's bad judgment led him to try to return via the east face. He dropped to the Notch and began what was the first descent of the Notch Couloir. He passed spots so steep and dangerous that he could not retreat. At the base of the couloir, he was forced to traverse a very narrow ledge hundreds of feet above Chasm Lake. The ledge was later named Broadway. The ledge took him to a steep ice slope which he was unprepared to climb down. He slipped and accelerated rapidly toward what should have been certain death. In desperation, he managed to throw himself around a projecting rock on the otherwise featureless ice. He broke his pocket knife trying to chisel out a foothold. Somehow, Lamb survived, and it wasn't until 1903 that naturalist Enos Mills repeated a climb of this route. The ice slope was later named the Lamb's Slide.

The year 1873 was very special for Longs Peak climbs. Anna Dickinson joined a U.S. government survey party headed by Professor Ferdinand Hayden. William Byers was also along for this climb. A route similar to the present-day Longs Peak trail was used, and at their timberline camp, the Hayden party named two of the surrounding mountains. Mount Meeker was named for Nathan Meeker, founder of Greeley. Meeker had been killed in the Meeker Massacre. His son Ralph happened to be along for this climb and was also Anna Dickinson's suitor. Hayden learned that Miss Dickinson had climbed Mount Washington in New Hampshire some twenty-six times, and he named the second peak Mount Lady Washington. Miss Dickinson's account of climbing Longs Peak focused on the climbing party rather than the climb. At the age of 31, she stood on the summit on September 13, 1873.

Anna Dickinson may have been the first woman to climb Longs Peak, but a far more interesting climb by a woman took place just a few weeks later. Platt Rogers and Judge Downer rode from their Greeley homes to Longmont and stopped for the night. The proprietor of the hotel said that a lady wanted to join them for their trip up to Estes Park. This was Isabella Bird who apparently had been eavesdropping. The men didn't want the burden of having a woman with them, but for some reason, agreed to take her sight unseen. What they imagined was a beautiful, vivacious young lady. The next morning, the rather dumpy Miss Bird appeared in bloomers and dispelled the men's dream of an attractive companion to escort to Estes Park.

The Colorado Mountain Club brought these old Arapahoe Indians from their Wind River reservation to Estes Park to try to identify geographic features using the original Indian names. The honored guests are Sherman Sage, second from the left, and next to him in the center, Gun Griswold. (Estes Park Area Historical Museum EP911)

The route to Estes Park was up the St. Vrain canyon, over a divide, down to the Little Thompson River and up to the head of Muggins Gulch. This was where "Rocky Mountain" Jim Nugent lived in a cabin. With his long hair, one eye, and a leather trapper's costume, Jim was quite picturesque. Jim presented Miss Bird with some beaver skins which hung on the side of his cabin. The party continued their ride down into the park proper where Griff Evans lived. Evans had a fenced in yard around his home, and beyond his fence, the entire expanse of Estes Park could be seen in its untouched state. The following morning, the visitors were treated by a visit of some bighorn sheep.

Evans ran sort of a tourist resort, and Miss Bird was rented one of his cabins for $8 per week including meals. The cabin was built of large hewn logs that needed chinking to keep out the cold night air. The roof was constructed of spruce poles laid closely together and covered with hay. The hay was covered with a thick layer of mud. The cabin did have a floor consisting of rough boards. Her living room was sixteen feet square and had a stone fireplace. Griff kept the fire going all during her visit.

As for Griff Evans, Miss Bird later wrote, "Griff, as Evans is called, is short and small, is hospitable, careless, reckless, jolly, social, convivial, peppery, good-natured, nobody's enemy but his own - a jolly good fellow." She commented about the merry life of laughter and singing which took place in the Evans home on a daily basis. As for Griff Evans' wife, she was a girl of seventeen and was raising four children. Griff was kind to his wife, but treated her like a squaw.

Miss Bird pushed the men to climb Longs Peak and to take her along. She recited her previous experience in mountain climbing and as a world traveler telling them about a volcano she scaled in the distant Sandwich Islands. The only mountain guides at the time were Griff and Jim. When Jim was hired to take Miss Bird up the mountain, Griff warned Downer to keep his liquor away from the man. This warning could have just as easily applied to Griff himself.

The party started out early the next morning and reached timberline that afternoon. They camped at a place later called Jim's Grove. Jim reminisced of his past life as the group sat around the campfire. He told the story of how a bear had disfigured him, costing him an eye.

At sunrise, Miss Bird set out on her pony while the others walked. At the Boulder Field, the pony was tied up, and the party headed toward the Keyhole. Instead of taking a direct route across the boulders, Jim led Miss Bird around the area, forcing Downer and Rogers to wait.

During the course of the climb, Miss Bird became so exhausted that she had to be pulled and pushed up the mountain. Using stimulating Jamaica ginger soaked in snow, they managed to get her to the summit Isabella Bird then became the second woman to climb Longs Peak. On the return trip, Jim insisted on repeating the indirect route around the Boulder Field again causing Downer and Rogers to wait.

By the time Isabella got to her pony, she was so exhausted that she had to be lifted on to the animal. The party camped a second night at Jim's Grove, then returned to Estes Park.

Although Downer and Rogers did not like having a woman along, they had to concede that she was a very gifted writer and an observant traveler after Isabella's book was published. As Rogers later stated about Isabella Bird, "Her physical unattractiveness, which so influenced us when we first met her, was really more than compensated for by a fluent and graphic pen, which made the mountains as romantic and beautiful as doubtless were her own thoughts."

Isabella Bird, an English author, provided detailed descriptions of early Estes Park and its pioneers including Griff Evans and Rocky Mountain Jim Nugent. She visited the park in 1873 and became the second woman to climb Longs Peak. (Estes Park Area Historical Museum)

A party led by famous explorer, John Wesley Powell, was the first to make a recorded climb of Longs Peak. They arrived on the summit on August 23, 1868, using an approach route from Wild Basin. (United States Geological Survey)

Lord Dunraven once controlled virtually all of the accessible land in Estes Park. His idea was to a make the park into a private hunting preserve. Much of the land, however, was obtained fraudulently by hiring men to make dummy homestead claims. (Denver Public Library, Western History Department F18404)

This was originally the Joel Estes homestead and eventually ended up in the hands of Griff Evans who sold it to Lord Dunraven. The property was improved by Dunraven and became known as the Dunraven Ranch. This site is now under the waters of Lake Estes. (Estes Park Area Historical Museum, EP632)

LORD DUNRAVEN CONTROLS ESTES PARK

The Right Honorable Windham Thomas Wyndham - Quin, Fourth Earl of Dunraven and Mount Earl, at one time owned and controlled practically all of Estes Park. His goal was to make the park his own personal game preserve. Except for the indignation of the early settlers at Lord Dunraven's tactics to secure the land, Estes Park might still remain in the hands of one family.

Born in 1841, Lord Dunraven could trace his origin back to a third century Irish King. He was educated at Oxford and became the lieutenant of a crack cavalry regiment. At the age of 26, Dunraven became a war correspondent for a London newspaper, but spent his leisure time hunting wild game around the world.

Lord Dunraven was an author of books ranging in subject matter from hunting, spiritualism, navigation, to the finances of his native Ireland. Among his books are *Canadian Nights*, *Hunting in Yellowstone*, and *Past Times and Pastimes* (the latter covering some of his experiences in Estes Park).

He had heard stories of exceptional hunting in the American West. In 1872, he headed west and arrived in Denver at Christmas time. In a Denver saloon, he listened to a young man describe his hunting experiences in a place called Estes Park. Lord Dunraven immediately began to organize a trip to reach the place. With two of his noble English friends, Dunraven headed up the St. Vrain River in a loaded wagon on the primitive road into the park. The party reached the top of Muggins Gulch and beheld Estes Park on December 27, 1872.

One of Estes Park's pioneer settlers, Griffith Evans, welcomed the Earl and his companions. Evans had discovered it was more lucrative to entertain visitors to Estes Park than to raise cattle. He had constructed some crude cabins around his ranch on Fish Creek. A cabin with two rooms and a fireplace was rented to Lord Dunraven and his friends. Despite below zero weather, the Earl unpacked and immediately went in search of wild animals.

Dunraven found the hunting exceptional with abundant deer, elk, and mountain sheep. Game was plentiful during the winter and spring, while in the summer, it was necessary to know where to look. The climate was also pleasant. The winters included long spells of good weather with intermittent storms. Cool breezes typified the summer evenings making sleeping comfortable.

Hunting had its dangers, however. Dunraven was hunting one July when he ran across a mountain lion. Dunraven was alone, having been separated from the rest of his party. When he saw the lion about to spring from an overhanging rock, Dunraven had just a split second to fire before the animal attacked. The lion was not stopped by the bullet embedded in its stomach. It had Lord Dunraven pinned to the ground about to bite into his throat when another hunter, Dr. Kingsley, came rushing up and shot the animal in the nick of time. Dunraven was shaken but got up and remarked, "...those mountain lions are blasted nasty things to meet when alone, you know."

Lord Dunraven returned to Estes Park in 1873 and again in 1874. Using his personal wealth, he decided to buy the whole park as a private hunting preserve. During his trips to Denver, Dunraven became acquainted with Theodore Whyte, who was also a member of Dunraven's 1873 hunting party. Whyte was hired by the Earl to purchase the land. The object was to file for all the land where there were springs or streams, thus controlling all the available sources of water. In turn, Dunraven could control the entire area.

The land in Estes Park was under the Homestead Act which excluded non-citizens from filing. A citizen, however, could claim 160 acres provided they lived on the land and made improvements. Whyte went about hiring men to make dummy entries on behalf of the Earl, and public officials were paid to remain silent about the matter. The recruits were hired, some for $100, with the understanding that they would relinquish their claims once they obtained title. The U. S. government was petitioned to survey and subdivide the land, and by May of 1874, around 4,000 acres had been filed on, with another thousand acres added by July.

Part of the Homestead Act required construction of a dwelling on the land. Dunraven and his agents made no real effort to comply with the law, and in some cases, four logs were laid out in a square. In the case of thirty claims, Whyte built a single shed and plowed 1/8 of an acre to satisfy the requirement for all thirty claims.

Lord Dunraven formed the Estes Park Company Limited, and all land was transferred from the names of the claimants to the company. Exactly how much land the Estes Park Company held is not known, but the Earl personally claimed control over 15,000 acres that encompassed nearly all of the accessible land in the park. Much of the land was held, however, without title, and fences were used to define the boundaries Dunraven wished to control.

A lot of money changed hands, and so many people were involved in the sham that it couldn't be kept quiet. A man camping in the park for his health learned of the land swindle and informed the Denver newspapers, thus unleashing a storm of protests against the Earl. In a grand jury investigation, thirty of the homestead filings were made under fictitious names and on none of these claims were the necessary improvements made.

The Estes Park Hotel, also known as the English Hotel, was constructed in 1877 by Lord Dunraven and was located on Fish Creek south of Lake Estes. Material included stone, brick and wood although the hotel looks like it is a frame structure. Dunraven eventually leased his hotel, the condition declined, and it burned to the ground in 1911. (Estes Park Area Museum)

When legitimate settlers began arriving in Estes Park, they put a stop to Dunraven's land grab scheme. The new settlers began to challenge the Earl's land titles, and they were successful in taking some of the land back. When the Estes Park Company sold out in 1907, it owned 6,600 acres.

For three decades, Lord Dunraven hunted in Estes Park and regarded it as his own personal property. He did not reside in the park continuously, but visited it each year. He typically brought relatives and friends with him to enjoy the hunting. Dunraven built a lodge on the North Fork of the Big Thompson River in a place now known as Dunraven's Glade. The lodge acted as his base for operations.

On the south side of the park along Fish Creek Road, Dunraven constructed a cottage for himself which remains standing today. At great expense, he built a magnificent hotel for his friends and visitors to the park. The hotel was called the Estes Park Hotel or English Hotel and was visited by a number of famous people during the years it remained in operation.

Wild parties thrown by Dunraven were the rule at the English Hotel. Lady Dunraven accompanied her husband to the park on occasion, but the Earl often brought a female companion. At one of Dunraven's parties, the noise was so excessive that it disturbed the other guests, and the manager was obligated to throw Dunraven out of his own hotel!

When the idea of a hunting preserve failed, the Estes Park Company began raising cattle. There was insufficient grazing land, and the summer seasons were far too short to keep the cattle fed. His stock business could not pay its expenses. The company, in fact, never paid a dividend. In 1878, approximately 1,400 cattle were reported to be in Estes Park.

Theodore Whyte was told that the Estes Park Company had to be self-supporting, and he resorted to cutting fences and driving the cattle over settlers' claims. The settlers, however, continued to encroach on pieces of land held fraudulently by the company. One homestead was located right in the heart of the Earl's property, almost in front of the English Hotel.

Dunraven became disillusioned with his attempt to control Estes Park. After the late 1880s, he did not return to his hunting grounds. It was estimated that he lost between $200,000 and $300,000 in the Estes Park venture. A lake that had been formed by damming Fish Creek in front of the English Hotel was allowed to wash away. The hotel became run down and burned to the ground in 1911. Whyte left the United States for England in 1896. The Dunraven property was sold to B. D. Sanborn and Freelan O. Stanley in 1907, ending a colorful chapter in Estes Park history.

THE MURDER OF ROCKY MOUNTAIN JIM

James Nugent, known as "Rocky Mountain" Jim, was a true character right out of the Old West. He had a knack for spinning yarns, and he made lasting romantic impressions on the women he met. He was a poet, mountain man, drunkard, and a liar.

History fails to detail where he came from, but Jim described himself as being the nephew of a southern gentleman, General Beauregard. He also told people that he was the son of a British army officer stationed in Montreal, Canada. He claimed he worked as a trapper for the Hudson Bay Company and the American Fur Company. He said he homesteaded in Missouri and fought with Quantrell. Other times he would tell about being a defrocked priest or a former school master. Research into all of Jim's claims has failed to substantiate any of them, and his past is truly a mystery.

During July 1871, "Rocky Mountain" Jim was making his way up the Grand (Colorado) River to Grand Lake. He left camp to visit a deerlick taking only his knife and revolver. As he came upon several deer, his dog ran howling out of some nearby bushes. The dog was closely followed by a large cinnamon bear with two cubs. The dog ran straight to Jim, and so did the bear.

Jim knew he was in serious trouble and began firing his revolver directly at the approaching bear hitting her four times. The bear bit into Jim's left arm at the elbow, crushing it. Next, the bear hurled Jim to the ground. Jim placed the pistol against the bear's body and fired his fifth shot. The bear, now very angry, released Jim's arm and bit him in the head, ripping his scalp to the bone. Jim collapsed into unconsciousness.

When "Rocky Mountain" Jim came to, he found himself alone in a pool of his own blood. He clothes were ripped to shreds, and deep wounds scarred his body. His right eye was hidden under his own scalp, and his left thumb was missing. Using his one good arm, he managed to mount his trusty mule and head to Grand Lake. He fell from the animal several times during the trip.

First to see him were two men living at Grand Lake. One of them thought he had been scalped by Indians. The men tended to Jim's wounds, and one of them left to find a doctor. About fifteen miles away, a doctor was located and returned to the cabin to help.

By August, Jim had recovered sufficiently to leave Grand Lake. A carbuncle about the size of a hen's egg covered his right eye. The right side of his face was badly disfigured. The bear's paw had slit the eyelid, permanently closing the eye.

There are no known photographs of "Rocky Mountain" Jim Nugent. This picture came from a painting done by Ken Keith and was first published in Over Hill and Vale Vol. III. (Johnson Publishing Co. 1971) by Harold Marion Dunning, a Loveland historian.

"Rocky Mountain" Jim headed over the mountains and arrived in the Estes Park area. Here he constructed a primitive cabin on the trail into the park at the head of Muggins Gulch. There he settled down and raised cattle.

Below Jim's cabin lived Griffith Evans in an old cabin originally built by Joel Estes. Estes discovered the park and was its first settler. Evans and Jim got along quite well for a few months, but their relationship gradually began to change as more visitors came into the area. It was not long before Griff Evans realized that he could make a better living providing food and lodging to the visitors than he could by ranching. Jim, on the other hand, was a born hunter and could not reconcile himself to these changes.

As early as 1871, Griff Evans planned to build a hotel for visitors to the park. Estes Park was becoming more popular as a place to hunt, fish, and enjoy the magnificent scenery. Evans began constructing cabins around the small lake formed by a low dam on Fish Creek. His wife cooked meals for the visitors, and he charged $8 for a week's board and lodging.

One of the first visitors to take advantage of this pioneer dude ranch was Isabella L. Bird, a well-known author. This Englishwoman was not deterred by her health problems and the primitive traveling conditions. She suffered from the effects of the removal of a large tumor from her spine. She endured periods of severe back pain the rest of her life.

"Rocky Mountain" Jim was the very first person in Estes Park Isabella met as she passed by his cabin. The barking of Jim's dog brought him to the door. Miss Bird wrote in her book, *A Lady's Life in the Rocky Mountains*, the following description of Jim Nugent and his cabin:

"Among the scrub, not far from the track, was a rude, black log cabin...with smoke coming out of the roof and window...it looked like the den of a wild beast. The mud roof was covered with lynx, beaver, and other furs laid out to dry, beaver pelts were pinned out on the logs, a part of a carcass of a deer hung at one end of the cabin, a skinned beaver lay in front of a heap of peltry just within the door, and antlers of deer and old horseshoes, and offal of many animals lay about the den.

Roused by the growling of the dog, his owner came out, a broad thickset man about middle height, with an old cap on his head, and wearing a grey hunting suit almost falling to pieces, a digger's scarf knotted about his waist, a knife in his belt and a revolver sticking out of the vest pocket of his coat. The marvel was how his clothes hung together, and on him.

His face was remarkable. He is a man about forty-five, and must have been strikingly handsome. He has large grey-blue eyes <sic>, deeply set, handsome aquiline nose, and a very handsome mouth. His face was smooth shaven except for a dense mustache and imperial. Tawny hair in thin, uncared-for curls, fell from under his hunter's cap and over his collar. One eye was entirely gone, and the loss made one side of his face repulsive, while the other might have been modeled in marble. In a cultured tone of voice he asked if there were anything he could do for me? I asked for some water, and he brought some in a battered tin, gracefully apologizing for not having anything more presentable. He was a true child of nature."

In his attempt to monopolize Estes Park for his own personal use, Lord Dunraven hired a man named Hauge to begin securing land in the park and to work with Griff Evans. Hauge decided he would like some female companionship while he was there. He had met a girl in Denver and hired "Rocky Mountain" Jim to ride down to fetch her. He gave Jim one hundred dollars for expenses and as a commission for this errand. A week or so later, Jim returned empty-handed. He told Hauge that the woman refused to go up to the park and spend the summer with what she termed "the English dog."

Griff Evans looks pretty harmless with his dog "Murphy" and was among the first settlers to take in guests to the Estes Park area including Isabella Bird. Evans purchased the homestead of pioneer Joel Estes. In 1874, Evans gunned down "Rocky Mountain" Jim Nugent. (Estes Park Area Historical Museum)

Naturally, this angered Hauge to the point that he called Jim a thief, a liar, and a few other things. Using the muzzle of his cocked rifle, Jim poked Hauge off his horse and forced the Englishman to retract what he had said.

The following day, June 19, 1874, "Rocky Mountain" Jim and William Brown where headed for Muggins Gulch. The two men paused at Fish Creek to let their horses drink. They were near the small cabin occupied by Hauge. The two men started to move away about the time Hauge and

Griff Evans appeared at the cabin door. Evans was armed with a double-barrel shotgun, and Hauge urged him to fire at Jim.

Various accounts differ in detail as to what took place next, but it is certain that Evans discharged both barrels at Jim without warning. Jim's horse was killed instantly, and Jim was mortally wounded. The attack took place so suddenly that Jim was unable to draw his pistol.

Some historians report that Evans was infuriated over Jim's advances toward his daughter. Others blame the alignment between Evans and Lord Dunraven with Jim standing in their way for complete control over the park. Other accounts blame heavy drinking by the otherwise amenable Griff Evans.

A doctor was out hunting in the general area and heard the shots. He rode over to see what was going on and found Jim with five bullet wounds in the head and face. One of the pieces of shot had penetrated Jim's brain, but Jim remained conscious. A piece of shot had gone through Jim's nose, splintering the bone. An attempt was made to move Jim into Griff's cabin, but Jim refused and requested that he be taken home. In the mean time, Evans rode to Fort Collins and got a warrant for Jim's arrest on the grounds that Jim had threatened his life.

After hanging on for several weeks, Jim was taken to Fort Collins. He filed charges, and warrants were sworn out for the arrest of Hauge and Evans. Hauge was released, and the charges against him were dropped. Evans, on the other hand, was charged with shooting Jim Nugent and was released with no bond set by the court.

Jim stayed at the Collins House, but was delirious at times. He hovered between life and death until he finally passed away that September. During this time, he wrote a detailed account of the shooting for the *Fort Collins Standard*. Jim Nugent made the following statement, "Evans is turned loose to hunt up bail...or jump the country, as he sees fit. Hauge is as free as the wind, and neither one of them are on a dollar of bonds." Jim also criticized the judicial system.

After the death of "Rocky Mountain" Jim, the charge against Evans was changed to murder. Due to lack of evidence, Evans was found not guilty at his trial. William Brown, who was with Jim at the time of the shooting, checked into the Collins House to visit Jim and was to appear at the trial of Griff Evans. Brown vanished before the trial began, and speculation holds that he was paid off. "Rocky Mountain" Jim Nugent rests somewhere in Grandview Cemetery in Fort Collins.

But what about the relationship between Isabella Bird and Rocky Mountain Jim? A number of historians have speculated that a romantic connection developed between the two after they had climbed Longs Peak. Presumably, when Miss Bird and Jim Nugent parted, they made a promise to each other. They promised that upon their death, the first one to die would appear as a vision to the other. Jim continued to write Isabella after her return to Great Britain. When she learned that Jim had been murdered, she traveled to Switzerland. One morning, as she awoke, Rocky Mountain Jim, dressed in his buckskin, was standing by her bed. He looked just the same as the first time she laid eyes on him at his cabin in Muggins Gulch. He bowed low to her and vanished. Certainly this would indicate more than casual relationship between the two.

The Denver Post *declared Enos Mills "The Father of Rocky Mountain National Park" for his relentless work to get the park established. Mills is shown here by the doorway to his homestead cabin which he constructed as a teenager. His daughter, Enda, operates the cabin as a museum, book store and library. (Rocky Mountain National Park 6226)*

THE FATHER OF ROCKY MOUNTAIN NATIONAL PARK

Enos A. Mills, without a doubt, was one of the great visionaries of the American West. Born in 1870 at Fort Scott, Kansas, young Enos was plagued by an allergy to wheat causing stomach problems and limiting his employment opportunities in this agricultural area. His parents visited Colorado during the gold rush of 1859, and his mother told young Enos of the wonders of the climate, high mountains and clean air. Enos was encouraged to leave home and strike out for himself. At fourteen, he traveled west over the vast prairie knowing that a range of great mountains lay beyond the horizon. He arrived in Colorado in 1884 and worked in Fort Collins. He helped Rev. Elkanah Lamb, owner of the Lamb Ranch, get his cattle from the plains to summer range at the base of Longs Peak.

Mills fell in love with the Longs Peak area and finished the construction of his own small cabin at the age of sixteen. In the process, he homesteaded the land. It was here in the tranquil setting, with Longs Peak at his doorstep, that Mills began to observe his new natural surroundings. The animals, flowers, geology, and weather became the focus of his attention and observations. Later, when he guided tourists up Longs Peak he instilled in them the same sense of wonderment and curiosity he had for his natural surroundings.

His ability to lecture was recognized when he was appointed as Government Lecturer by President Roosevelt. Along with lectures, Mills began to write magazine articles using his photographs to illustrate his articles. In 1905, his first book, *The Story of Estes Park and a Guide Book*, was published. This combined local history with poetry and stories about Longs Peak. No less than fifteen more books followed, leaving a legacy of his own thoughts and experiences. His daughter, Enda Mills Kiley, has kept many of Enos Mills' books in print. Among his books are *Wild Life in the Rockies, The Spell of the Rockies, In Beaver World, The Story of a Thousand Year Pine, The Rocky Mountain Wonderland, Your National Parks, The Grizzly Our Greatest Animal, The Adventures of a Nature Guide, Waiting in the Wilderness, Watched by Wild Animals, Wild Animal Homesteads, The Rocky Mountain National Park, Romance of Geology,* and *Bird Memories of the Rockies.* Along with his books,

Enos Mills had many articles published about wildlife, geology and the ecology of the Rocky Mountain region.

Mills joined Elkanah Lamb and his son, Carlyle, to become professional guides for tourists wanting to climb Longs Peak. Mills first climbed Longs Peak in 1885, the same year he finished his cabin. He ascended the mountain alone more then forty times in all kinds of weather before he felt ready to take others up the mountain. During his life, he led over 250 parties to the summit. Enos Mills is also credited with the first winter ascent in 1903.

Near the Enos Mills homestead was a ranch started by Rev. Elkanah Lamb. It grew into a modest resort known as the Longs Peak House and was purchased in 1902 by Mills. (Rocky Mountain National Park 3530)

Enos worked as a miner during the off-season in Montana to earn a living. In the process, he received an "education" in corporate attitude toward the environment. Realizing that the tourist industry was growing in Estes Park, he purchased the primitive Lamb Ranch in 1902. The ranch offered lodging to tourists, and Mills expanded the business. He named it the Longs Peak House, then changed it to the Longs Peak Inn. This allowed him to stay home, and Mills ran the resort the rest of his life. With it, he had a ready and eager audience among the guests for his ideas on the joy of nature. On the list of activities at the inn were nature walks, climbing, hiking, and bird watching. Indoor activities, such as card playing and dancing, could be enjoyed anywhere; thus these activities were not allowed. After a devastating fire in 1906, Mills rebuilt the inn to even higher standards. The cabins were equipped with steam heat and a private bath. He also added a nature museum to the structure. When business was slow during the winter, Mills took a job with the Colorado Irrigation Department measuring snow pack. He was ideally suited for such work, and it gave him a reason to continue to explore the Rocky Mountains on a paid basis.

Under the ownership of Enos Mills, what was once the Longs Peak House grew into the Longs Peak Inn, a major resort in the Estes Park area with special emphasis on the study of nature. (Rocky Mountain National Park 6212)

To provide shelter to climbers on Longs Peak, Enos Mills built the Timberline House in 1908. It had two rooms with bunks and a telephone. A caretaker cooked meals for the climbers. (Rocky Mountain National Park 6315)

Esther Burnell was an interior designer for Sherwin Williams and educated at the Pratt Institute. She was a guest at the inn, then worked as a part-time secretary, then a nature guide, and finally became Mrs. Enos Mills. Mills fixed up and expanded his own quarters in 1918 for his new bride. And when their only child, Enda, came along in 1919, Mills expanded their cabin once again.

According to contemporary author C. W. Buchholtz in his fine book, *Rocky Mountain National Park*, exactly who first suggested the creation of the park could be debated endlessly. Most historians, however, credit the idea to Enos Mills. Enda believes that her father first thought of the idea for a park while at his homestead cabin.

In 1892, Fort Collins pioneer and farmer John Coy proposed to the Colorado Forestry Association the creation of a reserve at the head of the major rivers in northern Colorado including the Cache la Poudre, Big and Little Thompson and St. Vrain drainages to protect the forest to ensure a clean supply of water to the plains. This eventually led to the creation of Roosevelt National Forest in 1905 coincident with the creation of the U.S. Forest Service. This was the first attempt at land management of the area surrounding the Continental Divide. The Forest Service policy, however, was management according to productive use and did not include the preservation of the natural environment. During this time, the Forest Service granted numerous permits to construct and operate lodges in the area.

In 1908, Enos Mills wrote a letter to H. N. Wheeler, local head of the National Forest, and asked about a proposed a game refuge of a thousand square miles being promoted by Freelan Stanley, Cornelius Bond and other businessmen. They belonged to the Estes Park Protective and Improvement Association, sort of a local chamber of commerce that realized that the tourist industry was what would eventually support the economy of Estes Park. Hunting had virtually eliminated all of the elk population east of the Continental Divide to the point where elk had to be reintroduced using animals captured in Yellowstone National Park. Mills continued to pressure the Forest Service about the game refuge that he envisioned as stretching from the Colorado-Wyoming line all the way south to Mount Evans west of Denver, encompassing the Front Range.

The game refuge idea grew into the notion of establishing a national park. After a great deal of effort, Mills was able to get Congressman Edward Taylor of Fort Collins to help him. A bill was introduced calling for the establishment of the Estes National Park and Game Preserve. In 1911, the name was changed to the Rocky Mountain National Park. Opposition increased from the Forest Service, who saw its power eroding and claimed that the area was being managed properly. Private property owners, who had land within the proposed park, were also against the measure. Mills and others could not accept the multiple use concept where cattle displaced wild animals and where the forests were under constant attack from logging. In 1912, the Colorado Mountain Club joined Mills in support of a park. The U. S. Geological Survey released a report in 1913 listing the unique geological wonders of the park, but included only seven hundred square miles.

This was also an economic issue. Since Enos Mills owned and operated the Longs Peak Inn where visitors came from all over the world to sample what was left of the dwindling wild west, his livelihood depended on tourism. The Protective Association also represented businessmen dependent on the tourist trade. Visitors, they pointed out, did not come to see logging operations or cattle grazing in front of their lodge.

The opening of Rocky Mountain National Park was celebrated in Horseshoe Park on September 4, 1915. The Denver Post *credited Enos Mills as the man who conceived the idea for the park. (Estes Park Area Historical Museum EP902)*

Mills used his ability as a speaker and made forty-two appearances to promote the park. He also used his pen to get sixty-four articles published in newspapers and magazines. This was in addition to the over two thousand letters he wrote. Mills spent much of his personal income on the project and was slandered and attacked for his ideas.

The first bill to create a park was introduced in Congress in 1913. It failed as did a second bill. But Enos Mills was present in 1914 for the reading of the third bill, and he was in good company. Also at the hearing to lend their support were former Colorado Governor John Shafroth, retiring Governor Elias Ammons and the new Governor-elect George Carlson. They all testified, and the bill was signed into law on January 18, 1915. The park's area, however, had been cut to 358.5 square miles.

Finally, one of the greatest days in Estes Park history arrived. Various officials, including Enos Mills, stood in Horseshoe Park on September 4, 1915, and officially opened Rocky Mountain National Park to visitors. Freelan Stanley posed with an undersized American flag held stiffly out at a right angle. The only figure which appeared to be relaxed, hands in pockets and without a hat, was Enos Mills. This was, after all, his home. Rain cut short some of the speeches, and maybe this was a sign that this natural sanctuary was not a place for speeches...at least ones made by mankind.

It was the end of a long battle and a tremendous victory for Enos Mills. The *Denver Post* gave him the title "The Father of Rocky Mountain National Park" and said, "It was Enos A. Mills who conceived the idea of conserving nature's wonderful workmanship in the Long's Peak region...and, single-handed, he set out to accomplish this result." Since that moment, the park has given millions of visitors the pleasure of seeing majestic mountains and wildlife, hearing elk bugle in the autumn, listening to loud water falls during the spring melt, and enjoying the still pleasure of the outdoors.

Enos Mills was injured in a subway accident in New York City. He returned home to the Longs Peak Inn where he passed away on September 21, 1922. He died of an infection which could have easily been cured today - an abscessed tooth.

The story of Enos Mills does not end with his death. His memory is kept alive by his daughter, Enda, and her daughter, Elizabeth. They have managed to keep several of Enos Mills books in print. After more than a century, the small homestead cabin built by Enos as a teenager remains standing. It is located eight miles south of Estes Park on Highway 7 just past the Twin Sisters trailhead and was opened as a museum by Enda in 1965. Although she was only three and a half years old when her father passed away, she has fond memories of him. He must have loved her dearly since among the Enos Mills Cabin Collection are thousands of photographs of Enda.

The Mills homestead was added to the National Register of Historic Places in 1973. In June, 1982, 180 people gathered at the Enos Mills cabin to join the Namaqua Chapter of the D.A.R. in a celebration. Enos Mills was honored by the dedication of a bronze plaque near the site of his homestead.

Enos Mills was anything but an armchair adventurer. He was a professional guide and led over 250 parties to the summit of Longs Peak. This is a shot taken by Mills of The Narrows on the Keyhole route to the summit. (Enos Mills Cabin Collection)

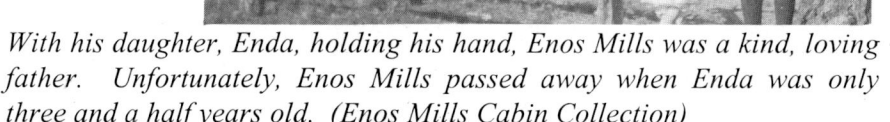

With his daughter, Enda, holding his hand, Enos Mills was a kind, loving father. Unfortunately, Enos Mills passed away when Enda was only three and a half years old. (Enos Mills Cabin Collection)

A. Q. MacGregor settled in the Black Canyon area north of Estes Park in 1874 and thought that a good investment would be a toll road from Lyons to Estes Park. Grading on what would be the first road to Estes Park took place during 1874 and 1875. (Estes Park Area Historical Museum EP400)

This toll gate between Lyons and Estes Park was destroyed twice by J. E. Blair, who was later joined by Abner Sprague in a lawsuit to open the road up to free travel.

(Estes Park Area Historical Museum EP463)

THE RILEY ROAD

Estes Park had the scenery, and during the 1870s, a small tourist industry was developing. What was lacking was a good road to the park. A. Q. MacGregor settled in 1874 north of Estes Park in a place called the Black Canyon near the rock formation known as Twin Owls. Within a year, he had an established ranch.

The only way into the park was the primitive trail constructed by Joel Estes up the North St. Vrain Canyon, and for the sake of his ranch and the economic development of the region, MacGregor decided to build a toll road. The Colorado Territorial Legislature granted him exclusive right to build and maintain a road from a point near Lyons to Estes Park and gave him ten years to collect tolls. MacGregor's wife invested $10,000 of her own money in what was hoped to be a good business.

The route selected roughly followed the one taken by Joel Estes and is today the route used by U.S. 36. For about three miles, it follows the North St. Vrain River then turns sharply to the north climbing up over a divide then dropping into the Little Thompson River drainage. From there, the route heads west to the top of Muggins Gulch and down into Estes Park. Pieces of this pioneer road are still visible today.

Work progressed on the toll road during 1874 and well into 1875 when it opened for business. A tollgate was constructed partway between Lyons and Estes Park at a strategic point where the road narrows as it crosses the Little Thompson River. Travelers could not avoid paying the toll of $1 for a team.

In 1882, this pioneer toll road was purchased from MacGregor by a group of Longmont investors. After the ten years had expired, somehow the toll company managed to retain control over the road. This infuriated frequent users who were dependent on the road. Estes Park citizens tried to get the road opened to free travel without success. J. E. Blair took matters into his own hands and one day refused to pay. He tore down the toll gate and continued his journey. Later, he was arrested and fined. He demolished the tollgate once again with the same result. He made his point, and was joined by pioneer, Abner Sprague, in a lawsuit against the toll company. The toll company was defeated, and without funds to maintain the road, it fell into disrepair.

Until the old road from Lyons was made into a U.S. highway, it remained dangerous and narrow. In 1902, an article appeared in the *Denver Republican* which said of the trip to Estes Park:

"On arrival at Lyons, he (the tourist) will find that the stage ticket sold him by the railway company obligates him to take passage in a three-seated, canvas-covered wagon, drawn by four quadrapeds, which at some antediluvian period, might have been characterized as horses, but which through abuse, starvation and over-work, now more nearly resemble skeletons. Crowded three upon a seat with heads almost touching the canvas roof, the sides of which extend downward preventing any comprehensive view of the landscape, and the weight of the load bearing down upon the springs until all elasticity is lost, the discomforts of the ride of 24 miles, consuming four to six hours...can better be imaged than described."

Well after the turn of the century, the Lyons to Estes Park road remained dangerous and narrow with few places to pass. (Estes Park Area Historical Museum EP403)

The Indians were the first humans to travel up the Big Thompson Canyon on their way into the mountains and plentiful game. Traces of their teepees and old trails confirm this fact. Leading a band of trappers, the intrepid Kit Carson may have followed the river in 1840. The trappers were after the numerous beaver and spent the winter in the Estes Park area collecting pelts.

The merchants in Loveland watched as the St. Vrain to Little Thompson River route through Lyons captured all the Estes park tourist traffic. A road was constructed over Pole Hill in 1876 to provide a direct route from Loveland to Estes Park and possibly attract some of the traffic. This route went up Dry Creek past Pinewood Reservoir. On the west side of Pole Hill, the route dropped into Muggins Gulch to join the St. Vrain toll road. Due to the steep ascent up Pole Hill, combined with elevations above 8,000 feet where the winter weather can be severe, this route failed to become popular.

In 1892, a small group of Loveland business men decided to try another route to capture the growing tourist trade. The People's Toll Road, Mining and Manufacturing Company was organized to firmly establish Loveland as the gateway to the Rockies. Their charter allowed them to branch off of the existing Pole Hill road at the crest of the first hill and down Dickson Gulch to the Big Thompson Canyon. They also could extend the road over the Continental Divide into North Park. From the canyon bottom, the road continued to Drake where it joined an existing road up the North Fork through Glen Haven and on to Estes Park. The owners charged a dollar to use this new road.

The steep and dangerous section down Dickson Gulch limited this road's appeal. Besides, when the river was high, parts of the road were under water and impassable. In the meantime, the St. Vrain route was widened and converted into a public road maintained by Boulder County.

Larimer County Sheriff Cornelius H. Bond got a petition drive started to have the Larimer County Commissioners finance a road directly up the Big Thompson Canyon through the Narrows. At Drake, the new road was to use the more direct South Fork rather than the route through Glen Haven to get to Estes Park. The South Fork was at this time untouched by any development. The petition drive was successful and the commissioners began accepting bids in 1903.

William A. Riley, a local grading contractor, won the bid at $27,000. It turned out that the commissioners only had a total of $24,000 in the treasury. A great deal of public attention was focused on the project, and Riley was authorized to begin work. He was given a year to finish the entire project, with much of the work in very rugged country.

By June 1904, the Riley road was completed on time. The commissioners were still short of the full amount and made claims that Riley had not properly executed his work. They found fault with minor things like the turnouts. Riley, however, was not a man to trifle with and boasted of operating the largest grading contracting firm in northern Colorado.

William A. Riley, at one time owned the largest grading contracting firm in northern Colorado, constructed the first public road up the Big Thompson Canyon to Estes Park. (Loveland Public Library)

The commissioners refused to pay Riley the full amount. Riley simply declared that the road was his private property to do with as he wanted. To further establish his control, he dismantled several bridges. He also joined forces with Loveland businessmen and organized the Loveland & Estes Park Railroad Company to utilize the grade. The proposed railroad was to carry tourists directly from a connection with the Colorado & Southern in Loveland to Estes Park.

A counterattack was launched by the commissioners by sending a labor force into the canyon to finish the road and open it to traffic. Riley repelled these forces and promptly began work on a house in the middle of the grade. The matter ended up in court. Riley won easily and received full payment for his work.

Riley's pioneer road up the Big Thompson Canyon would qualify by today's standards as nothing more than a rough, rutted, single-lane jeep road. There were few turnouts and no shoulders. The road was not much above the normal river level and was inundated during high water.

Newspapers of the day recorded some strange strategies to use the Riley Road. The stage coach from Loveland to Estes Park was granted the right-of-way in both directions. If a coach and a wagon met far from a turnout, the men on the coach would unhitch the horses from the wagon and walk them around the coach. Next, the men would remove the wheels from the wagon and lower the box to the ground. The wheels would be rolled around the coach. The wagon box would then be deposited on the hillside to allow the coach to pass. The wagon would be reassembled, and the two vehicles would continue their journey.

Completed in 1904 according to a contract with Larimer County, the road up the Big Thompson Canyon opened up another route to Estes Park. The county, however, withheld funds from the contractor, William Riley. Riley took possession of the road and dismantled several bridges until he got paid. (photo by Clatworthy, Estes Park Area Historical Museum EP405)

After more than a quarter of a century of use, the state of Colorado decided to replace the old Riley road with a modern highway which became U.S. 34. The highway was built in small sections to avoid disrupting traffic. Work began in 1931 and bids were let on the final section in 1936 between Drake and Estes Park up the South Fork. The last few miles were oiled in September, 1937 with the official opening on May 28, 1938. The opening ceremonies took place at the mouth of the canyon with Governor Teller Ammons giving the keynote address. He then applied a three-foot key to an equally oversized padlock. This was followed by an eighteen gun salute.

The new highway made it practical for the grandeur of the Big Thompson Canyon to be enjoyed by millions of people. It greatly expanded Loveland's tourist trade. But as the years passed, the canyon became cluttered with motels, guest cottages, cider stands, restaurants, shops and summer homes. Lost forever was the primitive feel the canyon once held for visitors.

Night came early on July 31, 1976 as a violent thunderstorm was spawned over the foothills. The storm remained in one place and dumped over eleven inches of rain in less than two hours covering over one hundred square miles. The enormous tonnage of water drained into the Big Thompson Canyon with little or no warning, and years of encroachment by mankind was flushed away. All traces of the old Riley road were also washed away.

This Stanley Steamer seems quite isolated in the Big Thompson Canyon. In 1910, this road would hardly qualify as much more than a jeep road with two deep ruts. Today, U.S. 34 follows this same route from Loveland to Estes Park. (Estes Park Area Museum E434)

STANLEY: HIS STEAMER AND HOTEL

Until 1903, Freelan O. Stanley had lived a productive life, and then he contracted tuberculosis. His doctor gave him a year to live and advised him to seek a high, dry climate. The 53-year-old Stanley and his wife traveled by train from their New England home to Denver with their possessions including Freelan's personal automobile, the legendary Stanley Steamer. Freelan had heard that Estes Park would be ideal for his recovery.

His wife and her maid traveled by train from Denver to Lyons and then took a conventional stagecoach to Estes Park. Freelan, on the other hand, wanted to test his steamer and drive to Estes Park. He tried several times to hire someone to go with him, but the site of a horseless carriage frightened all potential prospects. At the time, few people in Colorado had seen an automobile much less one that sounded like a steam locomotive.

Stanley drove to Lyons and stayed at Welch's Stage Stop located four miles farther up the North St. Vrain River. William Welch thought that attempting to drive up the rough, narrow, dirt road to Estes Park was insanity. Having lived there since 1893, he knew the road well. Besides, the car looked like a coffin supported on spindly wheels.

The following morning Welch watched Freelan take off up the steep road which had never felt the weight of anything but animal powered vehicles. This was also the first time a Stanley Steamer had been used in the Rocky Mountains. After an hour and fifty minutes of chugging along with an occasional water stop, Freelan reached the park. He walked into Sam Service's general store on Elkhorn Avenue and used the town's only telephone to call the skeptical Welch in Lyons. So incredible was the short time it took Stanley to reach Estes Park that Welch refused to believe what had happened. The store's owner, Sam Service himself, was summoned to the telephone to verify that Stanley was in fact physically in Estes Park and that his hissing contraption was there with him!

After a three month stay at the Elkhorn Lodge, Stanley's weight increased from 118 pounds to a respectable 147 pounds. He regained his strength, and Stanley and his wife returned to their Newton, Massachusetts, home. So impressed were they with Estes Park that they returned in 1904 and again in 1905 for a holiday in the mountains. In 1906, Stanley constructed a gracious home on Wonder View Avenue, and here he spent his next 37 summers.

Stanley teamed up with B. D. Sanborn to purchase a large tract of land owned by Lord Dunraven. The condition that Sanborn placed on his part of the purchase was that Stanley would improve the road from Lyons and would also construct a large, modern hotel in Estes Park. Using his talents to do a series of architectural drawings, Stanley settled on the Georgian style for the hotel. From 1907 to 1909, work progressed on the hotel using lumber from a forest fire in Hidden Valley. Originally, Stanley thought the hotel should be called "The Dunraven," but he put it to a vote among Estes Park residents. The "Stanley Hotel" was picked as the proper name for the structure.

In 1903, Freelan O. Stanley was forced to leave his New England home for a high, dry climate. He selected Estes Park and ended up being more than just another visitor. He was first to drive an automobile to the park, constructed the largest hotel in the park, and built a power plant which brought the first electricity to the area. (Estes Park Area Historical Museum)

Estes Park did not have any electricity, something that a modern hotel could not be without. Stanley had a dam built across the Fall River with a penstock to carry water to a hydroelectric plant to provide power to the hotel. He sold the surplus power to other commercial properties thus becoming the father of electric lighting in Estes Park.

In June, 1909, the hotel was ready for its first guests, and a convention of Colorado pharmacists was scheduled. The pharmacists met at the

Loveland depot. For the trip up the Big Thompson Canyon, Stanley had 21 eight-passenger touring cars ready. During his trip down the canyon, Stanley placed a full-size, realistic stuffed grizzly bear on a rock which hung over the narrow road. On the way up, he rode in the lead car and when he reached the bear, he yelled out and brought the caravan to a sudden halt. Startled and ready to defend themselves, the pharmacists soon realized it was a joke played by their host. Reviews of the Stanley Hotel placed it among the finest in the world.

What etched Stanley and his twin brother into history was their famous automobile. In 1886, Freelan and Francis developed a successful dry-plate photographic process. They eventually built a factory in Newton, Massachusetts, and worked on a means of loading a dry-plate into a camera. Francis became distracted in 1897 after he saw a primitive steam-powered car at a show. He believed he could design and build a much more practical unit and eventually constructed a small 350 pound prototype for $500. He boasted of how it was larger than any carriage he owned and since it was mechanical, would not balk at noises, did not have to be tied to a hitching post when it was not in use, and did not have to be fed. He drove his unit to Kennebunkport, Main, and also won a competition among other horseless carriages at an exhibition in Boston.

Shown in a cowboy outfit, there are relatively few photographs of Freelan O. Stanley, who avoided cameras even though part of his fortune was made in the photographic film business. (Estes Park Area Historical Museum EP218)

As its excellent performance became known, people came to the Stanley brothers to purchase steamers. Freelan began helping Francis by carving the wooden patterns for the castings so that the vehicle could be mass-produced. Freelan was good with his hands and a highly skilled violin maker. In 1898, the brothers produced twenty cars, and a year later 200 were manufactured.

Demand soared, and they had to decide between the lucrative photographic business and the automobile business. Their decision was to sell their Stanley Steamer plant. Freelan helped the new company get started by driving to the top of Mount Washington in an hour and a half, a feat not remotely possible with a team. Under the new ownership, the company fell on hard times and eventually receivership. For a song, the Stanley brothers bought it back and revitalized sales by introducing a new and more powerful model in 1901.

For many years, only Stanley Steamers were in photographs of the Estes Park area. They were powerful, rugged and had high ground clearance. The distinctive coffin-like prow, which contained the boiler, was a dead give away. (Estes Park Area Historical Museum EP467)

In the meantime, the founder of Kodak, George Eastman, found it increasingly difficult to complete with the Stanley Dry Plate Company. He purchased the company, the patent rights and began to manufacture a 4 x 5 camera with the Stanley logo on the front.

The Stanley brothers entered the automobile record books with a fast sports model. They broke the world's land speed record in 1906 on the hard sand beach at Daytona, Florida, with an official speed of 127 miles per hour. This was faster than any aircraft flying at that time. The car was improved, and the following year with a 1200 pound per square inch boiler, they reached an unofficial speed of 197 miles per hour. At that velocity, the vehicle became airborne and broke into pieces, but the driver managed to survive. This unofficial record stood for two decades.

A Stanley Steamer was a steam locomotive on wheels. It used four tanks; white gas, kerosene, water and oil necessary for lubrication. The fuel tanks had to be pressurized using a hand pump. To start the car, a torch was applied to an exposed piece of pipe leading from the white gas tank. This converted the liquid gas to a vapor. The white gas was used for a pilot light, and when the valve from the kerosene tank was opened, it ignited into an intense flame which was directed through a series of boiler tubes. A high pitched whine was characteristic of the main burner. After about a half hour, the boiler pressure was sufficient, and the vehicle was ready to go. With a toot of its steam whistle, the operator could direct steam to a pair of cylinders. The drive was direct and there wasn't any clutch or transmission. The car included a filler hose which could be used to pump water directly into the 40-gallon water tank.

The Stanley Steamer had a distinct advantage over internal combustion-powered cars of the time in terms of its ability to climb steep grades. Its pistons could supply ample low-end torque. So dominant was the Stanley Steamer during early Estes Park history that it is often the only horseless carriage shown in photographs taken in the village or on the canyon roads.

The problem with the Stanley Steamer was its complexity and the knowledge required for operation. The gauges had to be monitored constantly, and the car had a bad habit of flashing back when unburned fuel was ignited. When internal combustion engines were finally equipped with starter motors, the popularity of the Stanley Steamer dropped. The last one built rolled off the assembly line in 1925.

Could such a vehicle play a role today? Using alcohol, a modern version of the Stanley Steamer could run with virtually no air pollution leaving behind only water vapor. To save the environment, would people be willing to start their cars 30 minutes early?

In this 1907 view of early Estes Park, the only vehicles are horse-drawn carriages and Stanley Steamers. The Stanley Steamer dominated travel in the area for many years. (Estes Park Area Historical Museum EP405)

Stanley Steamers are shown in this 1912 photograph about to depart from the Colorado & Southern depot in Loveland for a ride up the Big Thompson Canyon to Estes Park. This was the most common transportation for tourists. The large touring car in the lead could hold nine passengers. (Estes Park Area Historical Museum EP437)

THE HIGHEST ROAD IN THE U.S.

In 1913, the Estes Park Protective and Improvement Association convinced the State of Colorado to build a road up the Fall River, over Fall River Pass on the Continental Divide then down to Grand Lake. In this way, Estes Park and Grand Lake would be joined, and visitors could reach Rocky Mountain National Park from both the eastern and western sides. Heading the Improvement Association were prominent citizens including Freelan Stanley and Cornelius Bond.

Convicts from the State Penitentiary were brought in from 1913 to 1914 to do the initial work before the project was turned over to a contractor. Cabins were constructed to house the workers, and local lodge owners feared they would escape. To speed construction, two road-building crews were used, each working from the opposite side of the divide. They met in September of 1920 to complete Northern Colorado's first road over the Continental Divide.

The Fall River Road was built primarily by hand and resembled many of the primitive mining roads of the time rather than a road geared for the tourist. It was very narrow with few places to pass and included sixteen switchbacks, some very exposed. Other switchbacks were so tight that the average car had to back up several times to get around. In places, there were grades up to 16%. Most of the Fall River Road was posted at 12 miles per hour.

On the eastern approach to Fall River Pass near the top a large 1,200 foot-long snow drift formed, and sometimes reached a depth of twenty-five feet. This required a great deal of expense to clear. At first, the Park Service would place a string of dynamite on the road just after its fall closing. When spring arrived, the buried dynamite would be set off to loosen the snow in the drift. The Park Service was eventually compelled to buy a steam shovel to perform the annual snow removal operation. The first few automobiles to pass through the upper part often had to be pulled through the drift by horses. Today, the road is not opened until it has dried out sufficiently.

It wasn't long before a better route over the Continental Divide was surveyed. The new route followed the old Ute Indian trail across Trail Ridge. Although much higher in elevation than the Fall River Road, the new route did not require the numerous hair-pin turns or steep grades. In

1926, the Park Superintendent walked the route several times and adjusted the initial survey. Through careful work, the grade was kept to a maximum of 7%, and in most places, the grade did not exceed 5%. By keeping the road on the south-facing slope, problems with deep snow drifts were minimized. The center-line for the future road was marked in 1927.

This clearly illustrates why an alternate route to the Fall River Road was planned over Trail Ridge Road. The Fall River Road was steep, narrow, and in some places, very exposed. (Estes Park Area Historical Museum EP422)

    The eastern part of Trail Ridge Road gains altitude by going around Hidden Valley and, without a sharp switch-back, curves around a ridge to double back over itself. On the western slope, parts of the old Fall River Road were used to a point where a new series of switchbacks was constructed to lessen the grade. The unused portion of this part of the Fall River Road was abandoned.

    W. A. Colt won the bid for the eastern section 17.2 miles long from Deer Ridge to Fall River Pass. He was a well-known contractor and had just finished the road to Bear Lake. For Trail Ridge Road, Colt established his construction camp at Hidden Valley. He had 185 employees with most of them working on the road itself.

The Fall River Road took seven years to build and was completed in 1920. This shows the beginning of the road in Horseshoe Park near the Lawn Lake Trail. One of the convict cabins can be seen on the right. (Estes Park Area Historical Museum EP455)

Great care was taken during construction so that the fragile alpine environment was not damaged to any more than necessary. Waste rock was hauled back down the mountain and not pushed off to the side. At the Rock Cut above 12,000 feet, no unnecessary amount of material was removed. When the contractor had to use dynamite, the nearby rocks were protected with wooden barriers so that lichen growth would not be harmed. In some places, the ground was stripped of all material. Tundra sod was used to cover these areas. Tasteful rock walls were constructed instead of metal guard-rails.

The first winter, 1929-1930, was mild allowing construction to continue until March; then, construction resumed in April. By the fall of 1930, the project was more than half done. The winter of 1930-1931 was a different matter. Due to cold weather and blowing snow, work had to stop in the fall and could not continue until the following June. The eastern portion of Trail Ridge Road was opened to the public on July 15,

1932. The old Fall River Road was immediately made one-way so motorists could drive to Fall River Pass and return down the newly completed Trail Ridge Road. This same trip can still be made today.

A 1,200 foot-long drift forms every year at the head of the Fall River Road just below Fall River Pass. A White twelve-passenger touring car is shown in the lead. (photograph by Clatworthy, Estes Park Area Historical Museum EP436)

High altitude was a problem for the workers. For eight miles, the elevation is above 11,000 feet and for three miles, it exceeds 12,000 feet. In places, the road was laid on permafrost. Care had to be taken to insulate it from the road surface least it would melt and the road would sink.

A Montana contractor, L. T. Lawler, won the bid for the 11 mile western section. The work was completed to the point where traffic could reach the other side of the park and Grand Lake in August, 1932. Work continued to improve the road south along the floor of Kawuneeche Valley to Grand Lake. Paving on Trail Ridge Road was not completed until 1949.

Trail Ridge Road is possibly the most spectacular paved automobile road in the U.S. with great views of the high mountains within Rocky Mountain National Park and the Never Summer Range. Below much of the road, the slope drops more than a thousand feet into Forest Canyon. Both elk and bighorn sheep are common summer sights. Driving Trail Ridge Road is often the one single event that visitors remember most about Rocky Mountain National Park. It is the highest continuous highway in the U.S. reaching an elevation of 12,183 feet.

This photograph was taken looking toward the rock cut near the highest point on Trail Ridge Road before grading began. U.S. 34 now runs from where the photographer is standing through the rock cut in the distance. (Rocky Mountain National Park 801)

Taken during the spring of 1927, this remarkable photograph shows surveyors marking the center line for the future Trail Ridge Road. Grading began in 1929, and the road was opened in 1932.

(Rocky Mountain National Park 2131)

This is what the future Trail Ridge Road looked like in 1930 while grading was under way. Elevations exceeded 12,000 feet with snow fall every month of the year. This limited how much construction could take place per year. (Rocky Mountain National Park 2757)

W. A. Colt won the contract to build Trail Ridge Road, the highest continuous paved automobile road in the United States. Because of the fragile alpine environment, Colt and his crew took great care not to cause any more damage than necessary. (Rocky Mountain National Park 2754)

LODGES WITHIN ROCKY MOUNTAIN PARK

The very purpose of a National Park is to bring people close to nature...to minimize human disturbances. A park is to educate the visitor in the ways of wildlife and provide a place for healthy exercise, fresh air, and renewal. During the history of Rocky Mountain National Park, the Park Service has had to make some difficult decisions in regard to the numerous lodges and businesses it inherited within the park's boundaries. Once the economic usefulness of these businesses had passed and visitors to the area could buy their film, gasoline, and food and find their lodging in Estes Park, the Park Service had to decide what to do next. One option was to favor some form of historic preservation or allow selected lodges to continue to operate. What the Park Service did, however, was to return the park to its natural state.

It is difficult to imagine what Rocky Mountain National Park was like between its founding in 1915 through the early 1960s since today it seems so raw and unexplored. Human activity, structures, and traffic are so visible in other places like the Grand Canyon, Yellowstone, Yosemite, and Grand Teton National Park. Rocky Mountain National Park was once quite similar and was dotted with hundreds of structures built before the park was created. Through methodical purchases, the Park Service has managed to buy virtually all of the privately owned property within its borders. It took decades, but the Park Service has removed the structures so carefully that hardly a sliver of wood, a piece of glass, or a rusty nail remains today.

Fern Lake, for example, was not always pristine. A man named Workman got permission from the Forest Service to build a cabin along the shores of this picturesque lake, a task which he completed in 1911. The cabin became a lodge and a business. Lunch was available, and the Fern Lake Lodge also had a store which catered to fishermen. When the Park Service got possession of the Fern Lake Lodge in 1958, all of the buildings except the lodge itself were cleared from this relatively remote place accessible only by trail. The lodge was left as a trail-side historical display of early accommodations. Vandalism of the old building forced the Park Service to burn the structure to the ground in 1976.

Well below Fern Lake, but still a three-and-a-half mile hike, another trail-side lodge called the Forest Inn was constructed. By 1926, there were fourteen tent platforms with concrete pads and a two-story main building where meals were served. The lodge was located in a beautiful place where the trail crosses over the Big Thompson River and where the water spills into a deep hole called The Pool. During the 1940s, the cost to stay there was just $5.25 per day including meals. When the owner reached the ripe old age of 86, he retired and sold the place to the Park Service. The structures were demolished, the debris hauled off, and the land restored back to its natural state.

This unsightly accumulation of structures once greeted visitors to Bear Lake. There were a number of cabins, an upper and lower lodge, a dining hall and even gasoline pumps. When the lease ended in 1958, the Park Service set out to restore the area back to its original appearance and all buildings were removed. (Rocky Mountain National Park 085)

Today, it is hard to imagine boats on Bear Lake and, on its eastern shore, a large lodge used as the Bear Lake Trail School for Boys. There were numerous cabins, a dining hall, a recreation building, and gasoline pumps next to a store. Bear Lake could not have given visitors much of the feeling of being on the edge of a wilderness. When the lease ended in

1958, the Park Service went to work removing every reminder that Bear Lake Lodge ever existed. Now the site is fenced off for restoration.

When one stands in Horseshoe Park to hear the elk bugle in mid-October or to enjoy a warm summer day hiking up the Lawn Lake trail or a dusty drive up the old Fall River Road, it is difficult to picture the two large lodges that once occupied this area. One was the Horseshoe Inn located immediately west of the parking lot where the road swings around for its climb up to Deer Ridge Junction. This lodge could accommodate one hundred guests and began operation in 1909. It was four-stories high and sat by an artificial pond stocked with hungry trout. Its end came in 1933.

The Fall River Lodge was located just east of the Endovalley campground at the foot of the climb to Fall River Pass. Built prior to the formation of Rocky Mountain National Park, it was eventually purchased by the Park Service and in 1960, razed. (Rocky Mountain National Park 185)

The Fall River Lodge was located at the western end of Horseshoe Park just east of the Endovalley camp ground. It was so wet that the owners had to drain the area first. Like all the other lodges, it was built prior to the formation of the park. Its owners probably witnessed the opening ceremonies in September, 1915 held not too far away. At the time the lodge was purchased by the Park Service, it could accommodate one hundred guests. The artificial lake was drained and all buildings were razed in 1960. The land was returned to the elk and beaver.

The Abner Sprague family homesteaded in Moraine Park in 1874 and eventually went into the tourist business with the Sprague Hotel. This photo of the main lodge building was taken in the 1880s. The Park Service went about the purchase of all commercial property in the park, and this structure was eventually razed. (Rocky Mountain National Park 2262)

One of the most interesting businesses in the Park was the Deer Ridge Chalet located at the intersection of the roads from Beaver Meadows, Horseshoe Park, and the beginning of Trail Ridge Road. It started as a store to purchase film and have photographs enlarged and grew to include a gasoline station, restaurant, rock shop, and lookout tower. It was never designed to accommodate overnight guests. The main building was moved down into Estes Park to become the Masonic Lodge. The rest of the structures were removed in 1960, and Deer Ridge was returned to the deer.

Moraine Park had three major lodges and several clusters of cabins for rent. The Moraine Park Lodge sat at the base of Eagle Cliff and could serve one-hundred guests at its height. The Park Service saved one of the original buildings for use as the Moraine Park Museum.

Also in Moraine Park was The Brinwood. It was at the end of the automobile road and at the trailhead leading to Fern Lake. The Brinwood opened in 1911 and as the years passed, nearly thirty buildings and cabins were added. It had hot water, electric lights, telephone and telegraph plus fishing, a tennis court and a golf course. After its purchase by the Park Service, the owners were given several extensions to allow them to continue operations. Finally time ran out, and the structures were razed in 1960.

After the Sprague family sold its Moraine Park facility, they constructed the Glacier Basin Lodge along Glacier Creek next to Sprague Lake. It was eventually purchased by the Park Service, and in 1960, all the buildings in the complex were razed except for the stables. (Rocky Mountain National Park 320)

The Sprague family homesteaded in Moraine Park beginning in 1874 with their holdings growing to include 640 acres. Ranching was the objective of the family but they fell into the tourist business as demands were placed on them for food and lodging by passing tourists. By 1880, a large building sat in Moraine Park called The Sprague Hotel. It could handle thirty guests at that time, but was expanded over the years. Numerous cottages were added along with out-buildings necessary to run the ranch. There was also a store and post office with regular mail service. Postal officials objected to the original name, Willow Park, since there were other Willow Parks throughout the U.S. Abner Sprague came up with the name Moraine Park for the two lateral moraines which formed the valley. In 1902, business had grown to the point where the Spragues took on Mr. and Mrs. Stead as partners.

The Spragues got out of the hotel business, and their Moraine Park lodge became known as Stead's Ranch. The Spragues tried to be happy in Loveland, but they missed the mountains. As a result, they opened up another lodge along Glacier Creek a short distance from the Bear Lake Road. A large lodge building was constructed approximately where the Sprague Lake parking lot is located today. It was called the Glacier Basin Lodge. The Park Service purchased the property in 1932 and gave the Sprague's a twenty year lease which was later extended. In 1960 after the lease terminated, all of the buildings except the stables were razed.

Although efforts were made by Estes Park residents to encourage the Park Service to save the historic structures at Stead's Ranch, all of the buildings were either moved or razed in 1963 including the Sprague homestead. The swimming pool was filled in with soil and the nine-hole golf course was returned to its natural state. The Park Service acted in a consistent manner regarding man-made structures favoring none and believing that what the public cherished most was a wilderness experience. This ended the era of lodges within Rocky Mountain National Park.

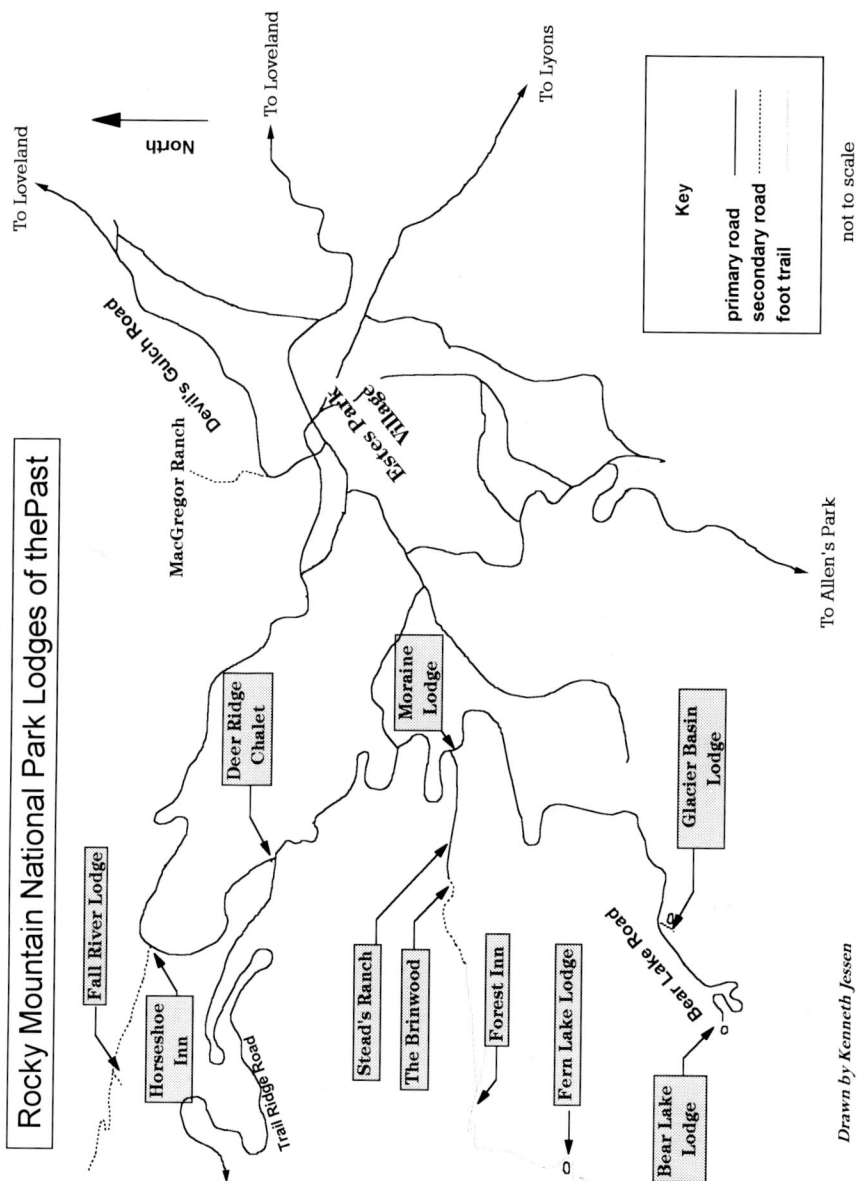

These tents and tent platforms were once part of the Forest Inn cluster and were located along the Big Thompson River near The Pool. This is where the Fern Lake trail crosses the river. Such commercial development did not fit into the theme of the park, and all of the structures which comprised this lodge were eventually torn down by the Park Service. (Rocky Mountain National Park 244)

This barn, part of the Stead's Ranch, would look fine on a farm, but in Moraine Park, it was out of place and interfered with the enjoyment of the natural beauty of the park. In 1960, all the buildings were demolished giving Moraine Park back to the elk and other wild life.

(Rocky Mountain National Park 333)

ESTES PARK VILLAGE

This undated photograph was taken from the top of Park Hill on the North St. Vrain road overlooking Estes Park. It was this sublime beauty which would attract tourists for years to come. (Denver Public Library, Western History Department F46506)

This 1902 photograph shows that the village of Estes Park was slow to develop. Nearly three decades had passed since Isabella Bird, one of the park's first tourists, stayed at the Griff Evans ranch. (Estes Park Area Historical Museum EP005)

By 1905, the village of Estes Park remained small, but this year the town was officially platted. (Denver Public Library, Western History Department F16613)

When Denver photograph Louis McClure took this photograph in 1908 looking down Elkhorn Avenue, the village of Estes Park was beginning to take shape, and even though there were a few tents, the town was more substantial. (Denver Public Library, Western History Department Mc1005)

By 1910, the Estes Park Village had grown to include stores, homes and hotels with Elkhorn Avenue now clearly defined as its main street. (Estes Park Area Historical Museum EP017)

This 1925 photograph of Elkhorn Avenue looking east shows an Estes Park more familiar to the modern-day tourist. Automobiles line Elkhorn Avenue replacing horse-drawn carriages and wagons. Numerous businesses consume practically every foot of space. (Estes Park Area Historical Museum EP027)

This is the Elkhorn Lodge in Estes Park as it looked in 1889. William James traded his homestead for this land in 1877 and entered the lodge business. Starting with tents, the Elkhorn grew to become one of the major tourist resorts within the village of Estes Park (Rocky Mountain National Park 1810)

Israel Rowe built this substantial cabin at the base of Mount Olympus in 1875. Rowe worked on the road from Lyons to Estes Park, accidentally discovered the Rowe Glacier, and also discovered Gem Lake. (Denver Public Library, Western History Department F85)

COLORADO'S WORST NATURAL DISASTER

In 1931, the Big Thompson Canyon was changed forever when the State of Colorado elected to replace the single-lane, dirt road through the canyon with a modern paved highway. This made travel to Estes Park far more convenient. Built at a cost of $3 million, this road became U.S. 34. The official opening took place on May 28, 1938, officiated by Colorado Governor Teller Ammons.

Although there were a few scattered settlements along the Big Thompson River, the construction of U.S. 34 marked the beginning of population growth in the confines of the canyon. Retired citizens took up residence to enjoy their well-earned moments of tranquility along the river's edge. Working families settled in the lower portion of the canyon like Cedar Cove and could commute to their jobs. The grandeur of the canyon was opened up for millions of tourists on their way to Rocky Mountain National Park, and it was a route far more scenic than the alternate route from Lyons to Estes Park.

Commercial development within the Big Thompson Canyon ran rampant, and practically every square inch became congested with homes, cabins, cider stands, Indian jewelry stores, restaurants, motels and curio shops. The primitive nature of the canyon was lost forever.

Legend has it that the Ute Indians avoided camping near the river on their trips through the Big Thompson Canyon for fear of a flash flood. During the early 1880s, a Fort Collins newspaper gave a brief eye witness account of a 25-foot wall of water suddenly coming out of the mouth of the canyon. Many more floods were reported over the years at irregular intervals, and the Army Corps of Engineers estimated that a dozen floods had occurred since 1864. These accounts, however, failed to slow development in the canyon.

On a mild, humid Saturday evening, July 31, 1976 moist air from the Gulf of Mexico collided with cool air from Canada producing thunderstorms up and down the Front Range. The people of Colorado were getting ready to celebrate the state's centennial anniversary the very next day. At this time of the year it stays light until 8:30 pm, but motorists found themselves turning on their headlights at least an hour earlier. A massive thunderstorm built up east of Estes Park, stagnated and did not drift east across the plains typical of most summer storms. The intense rain it produced was dumped almost entirely within the area drained by the Big Thompson River. In places, nearly a foot of water fell during a four hour period. It was a rare series of events which took place that evening as the storm reached a height of 62,000 feet.

The Big Thompson flood cut the canyon deeper in many places. Many homes and businesses were destroyed by the tidal wave of debris and water while others were undercut. This particular structure was saved. (photograph by Kenneth Jessen)

The Big Thompson River drainage is characterized by steep hillsides combined with thin soil covered by little vegetation unable to hold back a large quantity of rain. The ground became quickly saturated. The rain water flowed into small gullies, then into creeks, and finally into the river itself. The intensity of this storm was enough to dislodge millions of tons of soil and rock which became part of the flow. In the canyon, the velocity and weight of the moving mass was sufficient to rip trees right out of the ground. The combination formed a slurry of mud, debris and water which was amplified by man-made structures, especially bridges. The liquid mass, with a density of wet concrete, accumulated behind a bridge until the weight would cause the structure to fail suddenly. This would produce a surge which would flow down stream and collide with the next bridge. As each bridge failed, the intensity of the flood increased. When the flood reached the lower portion of the canyon and caused the sudden collapse of the dam for Loveland's hydroelectric plant, the liquid mass reached a height of twenty-five feet.

The force of the Big Thompson flood swept debris around behind the Nihart Motel, about 6 miles east of Estes Park, until it was packed solid to the ceiling. This structure was razed and today nothing remains to even mark its location. (photograph by Kenneth Jessen)

Once the flood picked up sufficient momentum, boulders as large as ten feet across were carried along. They produced a dull clunking sound, and any object which got in the way, such as houses, concrete walls, roads, and so on, were no match. Added to the debris were numerous propane tanks which were yanked free of their supply pipes to join the flood, hissing and clanging together, acting as battering rams. The escaping gas actually propelled some of these tanks through the water like a torpedo. According to witnesses, the sound of the flood was deafening, much like the roar of a jet engine or a wind storm or an approaching freight train.

The effect of the flood on an automobile, mobile home, camper or even a large truck was to first lift the vehicle up on top of the flowing mass, then churn it under, and grind it into an unrecognizable ball of twisted metal.

The water in the Big Thompson River began to rise at around 7:00 pm, July 31 and just below Estes Park, the Glen Comfort store was struck and destroyed at around 8:00 pm. An hour later, the flood struck Drake where the North Fork and the South Fork join. A second surge was created when the flood waters in the North Fork propagated into the main canyon catching residents and tourists off guard.

During the four hours of the Big Thompson flood, over fifty businesses and over four hundred private structures were wiped out, but none within the Estes Park city limits. But what makes the Big Thompson Flood unique is the 145 lives lost in the disaster, the highest death toll in the state's history. As for U.S. 34, it was virtually wiped off the map in the Narrows, leaving hardly a trace. And ironically at the Estes Park movie theater, "In Search of Noah's Ark" was playing the night of the flood.

Early in the evening a call came into the Larimer County Sheriff's office about rocks on the highway. This was nothing unusual during a rain storm, but soon, the Colorado State Patrol got a call about the entire road being washed out. Office William Miller was dispatched from Estes Park to drive down the canyon while Officer Littlejohn was instructed to come up the canyon from Fort Collins. Their supervisor, 53-year-old Sergeant Hugh Purdy was notified at his home of where his men were located and immediately got into his car to assist. Miller, in the mean time, reported that the stream was out of its banks and began to evacuate the homes along the river's edge. He then transmitted another message that the mountainside had slid across the road. When the water got up on the doors of his patrol car, he abandoned the car and scrambled up the canyon wall for safety.

Littlejohn was told by Purdy to turn anyone around that was headed up the canyon. Littlejohn turned on his flashers and used his loud speaker to tell people to evacuated their homes. People hesitated, however, not believing that something was about to happen. Littlejohn continued up the North Fork toward Glen Haven until he could hear the boulders rolling and grinding along under the weight of the flood. At this point, Littlejohn turned his car around and escaped.

Purdy went up the canyon toward Drake to try to assess the situation. At 9:00 pm he encountered a sudden surge of water and radioed the State Patrol to warn residents downstream of an impending flood. Just fifteen minutes later, he reported that he was stuck and in the middle of it. He then said he could not escape. That was his last radio transmission, and the mangled remains of his patrol car were found after the flood. Purdy worked on behalf of the people of Colorado up to the moment of his death and was the first victim identified after the flood. His body was located several miles downstream. This 26-year veteran left behind a wife and three children, his ashes were scattered in the Big Thompson Canyon.

Fred and Edna Woodring heard a distress call over their C.B. radio from their Estes Park home and got into their four-wheel drive International Scout to investigate. They drove down the canyon and at a washout near Glen Comfort, tried to plow through the water running across the road. The force of the cascading water, however, pushed the Scout sideways and off the edge of the weakened road. Horrified witnesses saw the headlights of the Scout pointed skyward as the couple yelled for help over their radio. The Scout bobbed along, then the force of the water rolled the vehicle upside down with Edna trapped inside. This was where she died. Fred managed to climb out and clung to the bottom of the inverted Scout as it floated down the canyon. A National Park Ranger, who had come down the canyon in a piece of heavy equipment to repair the road, threw out a rope to Fred. Fred could not reach the rope and was carried to his death, still holding onto the Scout.

At a point 5 feet below the top of the new road, horizontal holes were drilled into the solid rock wall of the canyon for tie back rods. (photograph by Kenneth Jessen)

There were other reports of cars or motor homes floating by with their headlights turned on and their passengers frantically waving for help. In all cases, the vehicles were churned under and the occupants later counted among the dead.

At the Covered Wagon Restaurant, nine patrons and employees heard the warnings broadcasted by the Colorado State Patrol over their loudspeakers, but simply stood around and watched the water rise and eventually surround the building. The entire structure, with its occupants, was picked up and folded into the dark, churning water. No one survived.

On the day following the flood, forty bodies were found and the next day, the death toll rose to sixty-nine, then seventy-two, and it continued to climb. A week after the flood, the death toll stood at 104, and a month after the flood, 134 victims had been found. On September 26, the final tally was reached with 139 confirmed dead including two police officers. Locked somewhere in the silt and debris, however, six more bodies remain. There were an estimated 2,500 people in the canyon at the time of the flood, either traveling to or from Estes Park, staying in one of the motels in the canyon or living in the canyon.

The end result of reconstruction of U.S. 34 through the Narrows is a flood-resistant, elevated highway designed to withstand a flood of the magnitude of the one in 1976. (photograph by Kenneth Jessen)

Rebuilding U.S. 34 was of great importance since it was one of two major highways linking Estes Park from the east. Estes Park motel owners could quickly feel the drop in revenue as a result of the national media coverage and photographs of badly damaged U.S. 34. Granted, the road through the Narrows was totally destroyed along with other areas of the highway, but little attention was paid by the media to U.S 36 through Lyons. As a result, the traveling public was left with the impression that Estes Park could not be reached except via Trail Ridge Road.

Colorado highway officials decided to construct a flood-resistant road through the Narrows which, at some future point in time, might save many lives. On Labor Day 1979, work began in the Narrows. A large portable drilling machine was used to penetrate down nineteen feet into the streambed or at least four feet into solid bedrock. The holes were set only seven to eight feet apart, and into each hole a 30-inch, heavy steel caisson was lowered. Welded rebar was placed into each caisson and then the caisson was filled to the top with concrete. Forms were placed along the line of the caissons and a four-foot high footing was poured. So much cement was used that a steady stream of cement trucks went up and down the canyon for nearly a year.

Large I-beams, averaging fifteen feet in height, were set into the footing. Welded to the beams were horizontal tie-back rods, solid steel and one-inch in diameter. The rods were inserted into the holes drilled into the canyon wall which went back at least nine feet into the solid rock.

On May 17, 1980, at the mouth of the canyon, popular TV newsman Bob Palmer kicked off the celebration to reopen U.S. 34. Other speakers included the mayor of Estes Park, a county commissioner, the Colorado Department of Highways Engineer and Lt. Governor Nancy Dick. It had been almost exactly forty-two years since the original U.S. 34 was opened.

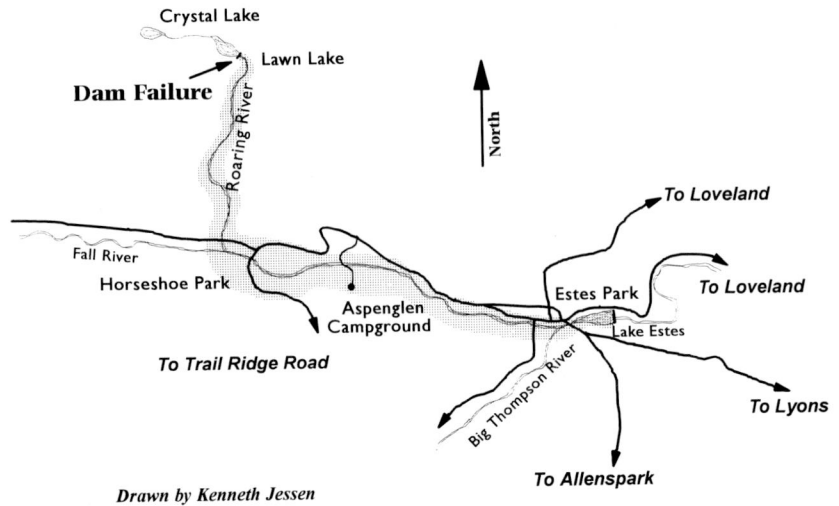

Drawn by Kenneth Jessen

The failure of the Lawn Lake dam caused tons of material to wash down Roaring River into Horseshoe Park burying many trees in the process. Some of the boulders were house-size. (photograph by Kenneth Jessen)

THE LAWN LAKE TIME BOMB

Steve Gillette, trash collector, was making his early morning rounds on July 15, 1982, and arrived at the Lawn Lake trailhead at 6:19 a.m. He heard a loud noise in the still cold air which he thought was an airplane crashing. Horseshoe Park was usually quiet at this time, and in a moment, he realized that the strange rumbling sound was a flash flood coming down Roaring River immediately above where he stood. He rushed to the closest emergency telephone, and at 6:26 a.m. alerted the Park Rangers. Steve's actions saved the lives of maybe a hundred people downstream because it gave Park Rangers and Estes Park police the vital time needed to evacuate the area. Of special importance was the Aspenglen Campground directly in the flood's path.

Steve was no ordinary trash collector. He had worked at the North Dakota School for the Deaf helping students with their studies. At the University of Nebraska, he entered graduate school and received an advanced degree in counseling and guidance. He had an article published in 1980 in the field of teaching the deaf. When he developed kidney problems, his doctor advised him to abandon his profession in favor of an active job, so he ended up as a trash collector.

The old earthen dam high in Rocky Mountain National Park was constructed just after the turn of the century and well before the park was formed. It expanded the capacity of a natural lake, called Lawn Lake, at the headwaters of the Roaring River immediately southwest of Mummy Mountain. With its limited storage capacity of 817 acre-feet, it served just fifteen to twenty Loveland area farmers through a water exchange program.

The Lawn Lake dam had been inspected in 1977, 1978 and 1979 all with recommendations that repairs be made and that the dam be watched carefully. State inspectors were spread pretty thin, and in the case of the Lawn Lake dam, they had to hike six miles up a steep trail to nearly eleven thousand feet. This took an entire day. To make matters worse, sometime during its history, the dam had been raised without state approval from its original height of twenty feet to twenty-six feet. It impounded more water than its original design allowed.

The failure was caused by "piping" or heavy seepage along the outlet pipe. The release valve was supposed to have been encased in concrete, but because it was buried, the contractor had gotten away with a shortcut. Once the seepage had started, the dam breached rapidly, and the water plummeted 2,300 vertical feet down the Roaring River streambed gouging out a deep trench and pushing large boulders down the ravine. In the process, Horseshoe Falls above Horseshoe Park was destroyed by the scouring action of the flood. Boulders, rocks, sand and trees were ejected into Horseshoe Park taking out a beautiful stone bridge. The debris formed an alluvial fan across the Fall River. As Fall River was impounded, a new lake, dubbed Fan Lake, was formed.

After racing through the Aspenglen Campground, the wall of water was momentarily stopped by Cascade Dam, which had been emptied for repairs. The weight of the mud, water and debris caused its sudden collapse, amplifying the intensity of the flood. A wall of water ten-feet high descended directly into the Estes Park business district and down its main street.

The Ponderosa Lodge was totally destroyed as the buildings were swept off of their foundations. Nicky's Restaurant and Resort was filled with water and mud with some structural damage. The Colonial Motel was cut off from the main road and fourteen of its cabins floated away. Hardest hit was the Fall River Village Mobile Home Park, where people's homes, filled with their personal possessions, were swept away to crash into trees and buildings downstream. The West Park Shopping Center was in the direct path of the flood and badly damaged. The historic Elkhorn Hotel at the upper end of Elkhorn Avenue also suffered damage as propane tanks, torn away from their moorings, hissed and floated with the flood acting as battering rams. One tank exploded upon impact with an Estes Park business much like a torpedo.

It was amazing that more lives were not lost, but there were three confirmed deaths with suspicions by the Park Service that a fourth was also killed. While still in their sleeping bags, two of the victims were simply swept away at the Aspenglen Campground. The Lawn Lake flood of 1982 damaged 177 businesses and 108 homes. In addition, eighteen bridges were taken out and the final bill was $27 million in lost property. With only half of its businesses able to remain open, Estes Park was hard hit economically.

Lawsuits were filed against the owners of the dam, the Farmers Irrigation Ditch and Reservoir Company of Loveland. The problem was that this irrigation company had practically no assets, and the final tally was a settlement for 9.5 cents on the dollar.

After the Lawn Lake flood, some serious thinking was given toward the safety of other dams within the park. High in Wild Basin, the City of Longmont maintained the Pear Lake dam, thirty-three feet in height, and the dam at Sandbeach Lake at twenty-seven feet with its arched concrete dam. The dam at Bluebird Lake, also owned by the City of Longmont, held back a thousand acre-feet of water and was by far the largest. It originally stood twenty-seven feet high, and was built of cement and rock. It was raised to fifty feet around 1916. Also, the potential liability against the City of Longmont could bankrupt the town.

The Park Service entered into a dam removal era starting with Lost Lake followed by Pear and Sandbeach lakes in 1988. The size of the Bluebird dam required the use of heavy lift helicopters to move heavy equipment into the area. The dam was slowly chewed apart and the concrete-rock mixture dumped into a hole and buried. The cost to rid Rocky Mountain National Park of its dams was $1.35 million.

Immediately following the Lawn Lake flood, Estes Park merchants were busy cleaning out their water-damaged stores. The flood happened in mid-July 1982, right at the height of the tourist season. (photograph by Kenneth Jessen)

The MacGregors were early pioneers who settled in the Black Canyon north of Estes Park. They first arrived in 1874, and the family is shown sitting outside their home in 1893 with the Twin Owls rock formation in the background. (Rocky Mountain National Park 434)

This was originally the homestead of William James, located along the Devil's Gulch road. James built this cabin in 1875 and later traded it for land owned by Reverend William McCreery. The Reverend and his family are shown relaxing outside the cabin. McCreery climbed Longs Peak in 1876, and at the age of 82, repeated the climb. (Estes Park Area Historical Museum 213)

HIDDEN VALLEY

by John Carr

The last large commercial enterprise in Rocky Mountain National Park was the Hidden Valley ski area, tucked away in a small valley. The small wooded valley had been logged at least twice prior to 1915 when National Park designation put an end to such activity. Estes Park pioneer, Abner Sprague cut timber there for his guest ranch in Moraine Park, and in 1907, a man named Fulton milled lumber for use in the elegant Stanley Hotel.

The exciting new sport of skiing and the amazing Trail Ridge Road converged in the 1930s in Hidden Valley altering the landscape and the economy of Estes Park. During this decade, skiers in the U.S. were just learning how to turn. Cross country and ski jumping had been the primary ski activities. The telemark and christiana turns, invented in Norway, were not widely known, and most who went down hill took a straight route, hoping for the best. A controlled crash was the common technique for avoiding trees or changing direction.

Ted Mathews, a long time Estes Park skier, recalled his astonishment in 1931 when he saw a Norwegian doing the sweeping drop-kneed telemark turn at a jumping tournament near Denver. From that moment on, Mathews became a convert to down hill skiing. While the new sport was thrilling, the intrepid enthusiasts had no choice but to trudge laboriously up the slopes they wanted to ski. For the fittest, six to eight runs was a full day. That all changed for local skiers when work on the new Trail Ridge Road cut across the top of Hidden Valley providing easy access to trails leading to lower Hidden Valley and the wide open bowl above the road dubbed the Big Drift. While snow fall is limited, prevailing winds blow snow over the continental divide into Hidden Valley providing good ski conditions.

In 1931, the Rocky Mountain National Park Ski Club was formed to promote local skiing. As testament to the level of talent in the club, two of its members made the U.S. Olympic team and competed in the 1932 Olympic games in Lake Placid, New York. The club sent a delegation to Washington D.C. to promote the idea of developing winter sports in

Rocky Mountain National Park. The Estes Park Trail boasted of plans to build a ski area that "...would rival any in the Nation."

A battle over the use of the National Park brewed. While on one hand, the Superintendent of the Park encouraged "...steady and vigorous interest in the healthful advantages of winter sports," he proved unable or unwilling to develop anything other than natural ski courses. This early struggle was over what constituted appropriate commercial development within the park and would define the next sixty years of Hidden Valley history.

As disgusting as it seems today, a saw mill once operated in Hidden Valley prior to the formation of Rocky Mountain National Park. (Estes Park Area Historical Museum EP709)

In 1934 Jack Moomaw, Rocky Mountain National Park Ranger and accomplished skier, managed to lure the U. S. Amateur Ski Association National Championships to Rocky Mountain National Park, perhaps the most prestigious event ever held at Hidden Valley. Moomaw cut a narrow path through the dense trees that plunged 1200 vertical feet in less than a mile. He dubbed it the Suicide Trail. A local skier, J. J. Duncan, took top honors and was crowned world champion in a race that drew competitors from across the nation. Ted Mathews broke his back during the event after smashing into a tree. The precipitous trail terrified many skiers use to more open terrain.

Skiing was still a matter of hiking up and skiing down until two high school boys installed a home made rope tow in 1941. But it wasn't until after World War II that skiing at Hidden Valley went into high gear when a veteran of the Tenth Mountain Division, George Hurt, built and operated three rope tows and a lunch shack. The popularity of down hill skiing bloomed throughout the nation after the war, and the Estes Park Winter Sports Club spearheaded an effort to modernize their local skiing facilities. A prospectus on the development of a modern ski area in Hidden Valley was submitted to Congress. In 1955, despite opposition from the National Park Service, Hidden Valley Winter Use Area opened. A new lodge was constructed, parking expanded, new lifts installed and a bus service initiated to carry skiers to upper Hidden Valley. Throughout the 50s, 60s and 70s, Hidden Valley operated a robust ski school. The ski area also maintained a platter slide, toboggan run, and a skating rink. In the scheme of ski areas throughout Colorado, Hidden Valley established a reputation as one of the premier small family oriented ski resorts.

In 1972, a modern chair lift was installed directly up the valley to transport skiers to upper Hidden Valley. Over the next five years, Hidden Valley grew to include a three story lodge, five lifts and employed one hundred people. Locals regarded the ski area as a great community asset. However, the Park Service made it clear that its feelings about the ski area were much different. A 1975 study concluded that high winds, marginal terrain, insufficient snow fall and an accident rate four times the national average made Hidden Valley unsuitable as a ski area. Because of this study and opposition to the ski area from environmentalists, the 1976 Park Service Master Plan concluded that Hidden Valley would be shut down when "alternative facilities become available."

As the Park Service had done with all other privately owned assets within the Park, it bought the ski area in 1977. This sealed the fate of Hidden Valley. The Park Service insisted the popular chair lift be removed, citing high winds and what it felt was a negative visual impact on the environment. Management of the ski area was handed over to the Estes Valley Recreation and Parks District. Over the next fifteen years Parks District struggled to operate the ski area profitably. Persistent management problems, competition from modern resorts, and environmental restrictions conspired against the ski area, and in the mid-1980s, the Park Service vetoed a plan to modernize and revitalized the ski area. The Park Service argued that the scheme was too costly, and that new runs and chair lifts contradicted its mandate to preserve the natural condition of the Park.

Mounting losses frustrated Estes Park residents, and without the ability to modernize, local officials questioned the viability of the area. On April 8, 1990, a headline in the local paper read, "EVRPD Quits Ski Business." In 1991, Hidden Valley was closed ending the last major commercial operation within the Park.

Hidden Valley was really two separate ski areas. The Drift required above average skill, and there were many days with weather conditions and wind slab (created by blowing snow) made skiing marginal. The lower area was well suited for the beginner, but lacked a variety of intermediate runs.

Remarkably, the history of skiing in Hidden Valley has come full circle. In the 1930s, skiers shuttled up and down Trail Ridge Road to ski the lower portion of the valley or climbed up the Drift for bowl skiing. Nearly seventy years later, skiers undaunted by the closure of the ski area and the removal of the lifts, still ski at Hidden Valley all winter. The equipment has changed and so has the clothing, but the love of skiing Hidden Valley endures.

The Hidden Valley ski area, shown during the winter of 1955-1956, had a wonderful lodge complete with a cafeteria, first aid room, ski rental area, snack bar and a viewing area. (Estes Park Area Museum)

BIBLIOGRAPHY

BOOKS

Bird, Isabella L. *A Lady's Life in the Rocky Mountains.* Norman: University of Oklahoma, 1960 (reprint of 1860 original work)
Buchholtz, C. W. *Rocky Mountain National Park.* Boulder: Colorado Associated University Press, 1983.
Dunning, Harold M. *Over Hill and Vale* (vol. I.). Boulder: Johnson Publishing Co., 1956, pp 99 - 130.
Foscue, Edwin J. and Louis O. Quam. *Estes Park Resort in the Rockies.* Dallas: University Press in Dallas, 1949.
Hawthorne, Hildegarde and Ester Burnell Mills. *Enos Mills of the Rockies.* New York: Houghton Mufflin Co., 1935.
Little Nature Studies of Estes Park. Estes Park: Estes Park Women's Club, no date.
Mills, Enos A. *Adventures of a Nature Guide.* Friendship, WI: New Past Press, 1990 (reprint of original).
Osterwald, Doris B. *Rocky Mountain Splendor.* Lakewood: Western Guideways, 1989.
Pedersen, Henry F. Jr. *The McGraw Ranch.* self-published, 1990.
Pedersen, Henry F. Jr. *Those Castles of Wood.* self-published, 1993.
Trimble, Stephen. *Longs Peak - a Rocky Mountain Chronicle.* Estes Park: Rocky Mountain Nature Association, 1984, pp 58 - 71.
Watrous, Ansel. *History of Larimer County, Colorado.* Courier Publishing Co., 1911, pp 174 - 188.

BOOKLETS

Bancroft, Caroline. *Estes Park and Trail Ridge.* Boulder: Johnson Publishing Co., 1968.
Canning, Anne Smedley. *Early Estes Park.* self-published, 1990.
Dunning, Harold M. *History of Estes Park.* Boulder: Johnson Publishing Co., 1967.
Hick, Dave. *Estes Park from the Beginning.* Denver: Egan Printing, 1976.
Kaye, Glen. *Trail Ridge.* Rocky Mountain Nature Association, 1982.
McComb, David. *Big Thompson: Profile of a Natural Disaster.* Boulder: Pruett Publishing Company, 1980.
Mills, Enos A. *Early Estes Park.* Denver: A. B. Hirsheld, 1911 (new copyright by Ester Mills, 1939).

Nesbit, Paul. *Paul Nesbit's Longs Peak*. Halstead, Kansas: Mills Publishing Co., 1990 (new copyright).
Pedersen, Henry F. Jr. *Sadness in Sunshine*. self-published, 1995.
Prosser, Glenn. *The Saga of Black Canyon*. self-published, 1971.
Stauffer, Ruth. *This was Estes Park*. Estes Park: Estes Park Area Historical Museum, 1976.
The Big Thompson Disaster, Grant Judkins, editor. Loveland: Lithographic Press, 1976.

NEWSPAPER ARTICLES - general

"Dunraven Holdings Bought" *Denver Republican*, April 4, 1903.
"Jim Nugent Dies' *Rocky Mountain News,* September 15, 1874.
"Mountain Jim" *Rocky Mountain News,* July 24, 1874.
"Sold for a Yoke of Oxen" *Rocky Mountain News*, September 15, 1874.
Tomlinson, John. letter to the editor, *Denver Republican*, July 10, 1902.

NEWSPAPER ARTICLES - Lawn Lake flood

"Cleanup continues in Estes" *Reporter-Herald*, August 18, 1982.
Dixon, Susan "Dick Approves request for Disaster Aid" *Reporter-Herald*, July 19, 1982, p 1.
Dixon, Susan. "Official to set up flood relief center in Estes" *Reporter-Herald,* July 23, 1982, p 1.
"Estes Flood" *Reporter-Herald,* July 16, 1982, p 9.
Farrell, John Alogsius, Bill McBean and Kit Miniclier. "4 Believed Dead in Flood" *Denver Post,* July 16, 1982, p 1A.
Farrell, John Alogsius and Tom Coakley. "Dreams go awash in Flash of Disaster" *Denver Post,* p 1A
"Flood recovery comes slowly for Estes Park couple" *Reporter-Herald,* August 11, 1982, p 7.
McBeam, Bill "Flood Victims body Found; 3 others sought" *Denver Post*, July 17, 1987, p 1A.
McBean, Bill. "Residents Optimistic: Vital Tourist Season can still be Revived" *Denver Post,* July 16, 1982, p18A.
McGrath "Body of flood victim found; 5 still missing" *Reporter-Herald*, July 17/18, 1982, p 1.
Obereigner, Dagmar. "Ditch Company Stockholders Register Uncertainty" *Reporter-Herald,* July 21, 1982, p 3.
Obereigner, Dagmar. "Big Thompson river drainages contains 8 high-hazard dams" *Reporter-Herald,* July 27, 1982, p 1.

Obereigner, Dagmar. "First Suit Filed in Estes Flood" *Reporter-Herald,* July 24/25, 1982.
Obereigner, Dagmar. "Cleanup continues in Estes; 4 presumed dead" *Reporter-Herald,* July 16, 1982, p 1.
Orr, Becky. "Question of Liability remains unanswered..." *Reporter-Herald,* July 16, 1982, p 1.
Petitt, Kep "Flood waters frustrate residents, tourists" *Reporter-Herald,* July 15, 18982, p 1.
"Reuteman, Rob "Estes Flood hero is unlikely Trashman" *Reporter-Herald,* July 24/25, 1982
Taylor, Jack "Dam Inspections found Problems" *Denver Post,* July 16, 1982, p 1A.
"Wall of water roars in Estes Park' *Reporter-Herald,* July 15, 1982, p 1.
"Workers find second body in flood debris" *Reporter-Herald,* July 21, 1982, p 1.

NEWSPAPER ARTICLES - Big Thompson flood

Bouton, Jay. "Guardsman: 'They Won't Find All The Bodies for Months'," *Reporter-Herald,* August 3, 1976, p 2.
Bouton, Jay. "River Level Highest Ever Recorded at Big T Narrows," *Reporter-Herald,* August 2, 1976, p 3.
Brimberg, Judith. "Stretch of U.S. 34 Reverts to River," *Denver Post,* August 2, 1976, p 11.
Ewegen, Bob. "Tragedy Haunts Survivors'" *Denver Post,* August 2, 1976, p 42
"Flood roar down Thompson, Poudre," Fort Collins *Coloradoan,* August 1, 1976, p 1.
"He Lost His Life Over a Damn Hog," *Reporter-Herald,* August 3, 1976, p 7.
Lewis, Springfield. "For Evacuation Helicopter, 'Like Flying Down a Tunnel'," *Reporter-Herald,* August 3, 1976, p 7.
Myers, Bill. "Many Who Heard Warning of Flood Stay to Meet Death," *Denver Post,* August 2, 1976, p 11
Myers, Bill. "60 Die; Hundreds Stranded,"*Denver Post,* August 2, 1976, p 1.
"Oh God, Don't Let It Rain Nay More, *Reporter-Herald,* August 3, 1976, p 5.
Pfeiffenberger, John. "Death Estimates Now Nearing 100," *Reporter-Herald,* August 3, 1976, p 1.
Pfeiffenberger, John. "Flood Toll 64, Still Rising; National Disaster Area Declared," *Reporter-Herald,* August 2, 1976, p 1.
"Temporary Post Offices Set Up in Loveland," *Reporter-Herald,* August 3, 1976, p 5.

INDEX

Allen, Alonzo 6
Ammons, Elias 28
Bear Lake Lodge 50
Bear Lake Lodge 50
Big Thompson Canyon 35, 61
Big Thompson Canyon - road 35, 36
Bird, Isabella 9, 19
Bird, Isabella 11
Blair, J. E. 34
Bond, Cornelius 33
Brinwood, The 53
Brown, William 20
Buchholtz, C. W. 1, 26
Burnell, Esther 26
Byers, William N. 2, 6
Byers, William N. 6
Carson, Kit 1, 33
Colorado Mountain Club 5, 27
Colt, W. A. 44
Covered Wagon Restaurant 66
Coy, John 26
Deer Ridge Chalet 52
Dick, Nancy 67
Dickinson, Anna 8
Drake 64
Duncan, J.J. 74
Downer, Judge 8
Dunraven, Lord or Earl of 13, 38
Eastman, George 40
Elkhorn Lodge 37
Elkhorn Lodge 60
Estes, Joel 1, 6, 12
Estes, Joel 3

Estes Park 42, 57, 58, 59
Estes Park Company Limited 14
Estes Park Hotel 15
Evans, Griff 10, 13, 18
Evans, Griff 20
Fall River Lodge 51
Fall River Lodge 51
Fall River Road 43
Fall River Road 44, 45, 46
Fern Lake Lodge 49
Forest Inn 49
Forest Inn 56
Glacier Basin Lodge 54
Glacier Basin Lodge 53
Gillett, Steve 69
Griswold, Gun 5
Griswold, Gun 9
Gun, Old Man 5
Hayden, Ferinand 8
Hidden Valley 44, 73
Hidden Valley Ski Area 73
Horseshoe Inn 51
Hurt, George 75
Keplinger, L. W. 7
Enda Mills - see Enda Mills
King, Clarence 8
Lamb, Carlyle 24
Lamb, Elkanah 8, 23
Lamb, Elkanah 7
Lawler, L. T. 46
Lawn Lake 69
Long, Stephen 5
Longs Peak House 24
Longs Peak Inn 25
Loveland 42
Loveland & Estes Park Railroad Co. 34

80

MacGregor, A. Q. 31
Mathews, Ted 73
Meeker, Nathan 9
Miller, William 64
Mills, Elizabeth 28
Mills, Enda 28
Mills, Enda 29
Mills, Enos A. 8, 23
Mills, Enos A. 22, 29
Moomaw, Jack 73
Moraine Lodge 53
National Register of Historic Places 28
Nicky's Restaurant and Resort 70
Nihart Motel 63
North St. Vrain Road 30, 32, 57
Nugent, "Rocky Mountain" Jim 9, 17
Nugent, "Rocky Mountain" Jim 18
Palmer, Bob 67
Pole Hill 33
Ponderosa Lodge 70
Powell, John Wesley 5, 6
Purdy, Hugh 64
Riley, William A. 33
Riley, William A. 34
Rocky Mountain National Park - opening 31
Rocky Mountain National Park - opening 27
Rocky Mountain National Park Ski Club 73
Rogers, Platt 8
Rowe, Israel - cabin 60
Sage, Sherman 5

Sage, Sherman 9
Sanborn, B. D. 16, 38
Shafroth, John 28
Sprague, Abner 31, 52, 53, 54
Sprague Hotel 54
Sprague Hotel 52
Stanley, Freelan O. 16, 26, 37
Stanley, Freelan O. 38, 39
Stanley Steamer 39
Stanley Steamer 40, 42
Steads Ranch 54
Steads Ranch 56
Sumner, Jack 6
Taylor, Edward 26
Timberline House 25
Trail Ridge Road 44, 73
Trail Ridge Road 47, 48
U.S. 34 36, 61, 67
U.S. 34 65, 66
Welch, William 37
Wheeler, H. N. 26
Whyte, Theodore 14
Woodring, Fred and Edna 65

ABOUT KENNETH JESSEN

Kenneth Jessen works for Hewlett-Packard in Loveland as an engineer and has been there for thirty years. During that time, he has held a variety of positions and is currently a program manager.

Ken is author of five published books including *Bizarre Colorado*, *Eccentric Colorado* and *Colorado Gunsmoke*. In addition to this booklet on Estes Park, Ken has had three other booklets published including *Built to Haul Sugar Beets*, *Trolley Cars of Fort Collins*, and *The Wyoming/Colorado Railroad*. Ken, with well over 400 articles to his credit, writes a weekly column on ghost towns for several newspapers and is Contributing Editor for *Colorado Time-Table*. He has also written for *Colorado Heritage*, the publication of the Colorado Historical Society. In conjunction with his writing, he has appeared on a number of radio and television shows.

Ken is one of the founders and the past president of The Western Outlaw-Lawman History Association. In addition, Ken has served on the advisory board for the National Association for Outlaw and Lawman History and the Outlaw Trail History Association. Ken is widely published in the field of Western history and belongs to a variety of organizations including The Westerners, the Colorado Historical Society, the San Luis Historical Society and the Rocky Mountain Railroad Club. He is a life member of the Colorado Railroad Museum.

Ken's education includes a BSEE and MBA from the University of Utah in Salt Lake City. Ken enjoys photography, traveling, hiking, and skiing in the Rocky Mountain West. Ken and his wife Sonje have three sons, Todd, Chris, and Ben.